S0-AHH-854

Scott
To a beginning!

You're the Buyer

You Negotiate It!

Best Wishes

by

Robert Menard

Robert Menard
Sept 2010

This book is a work of non-fiction.
Names of people and places have been
changed to protect their privacy.

© 2005 by Robert Menard. All rights reserved.
Cover Art by Jeff Pimental.

No part of this book may be reproduced, stored in a retrieval system,
or transmitted by any means, electronic, mechanical, photocopying,
recording, or otherwise, without written permission from the author.

ISBN: 1-4184-2624-5 (e-book)
ISBN: 1-4184-2625-3 (Paperback)
ISBN: 1-4184-2626-1 (Dust Jacket)

Library of Congress Control Number: 2004090872

This book is printed on acid free paper.

Second Printing
Printed in the United States of America
Dallas, TX

Dedication

This book represents the sum of many business experiences that have shaped my professional life since I began in business shortly after college. Most of these experiences were pleasant, some were nasty, but all were educational. Among the greatest lessons I have ever learned are these two:

1. For all business successes, a great part of the credit is due to others. Their efforts and their contributions in sweat, genius, and inspiration contribute far more than we are often willing to admit.

2. For most all business failures, the greatest part of the blame is due to the person whose reflection you find in the dressing mirror every morning.

I dedicate this book to all those, friend and foe, supporter and saboteur alike, who have contributed to the patchwork that makes up a lifetime and a career. Without you, this effort would not have been worthwhile.

In Special Honor

Among the greatest influences upon one's lifelong journey are those closest to us. Their patience, counsel, support, gratitude, approval and love are so prevalent in our landscape that we do not often appreciate the land, the stable footing that they so willingly provide. Without them, no creation, no success of any kind would be possible.

Among these people were my father, Robert A. Menard, who gave me a desire for education, self reliance, and a will to succeed. My wife Meg, a loving companion has given me the wisdom, motivation and love which has made every endeavor possible. My children, Kevin, Carrie, and Brigitte, have all been treasures of the heart. Love your children as if this were your last day together.

Foreword

This book will help develop skills in negotiation, the most valuable workplace skills of anyone involved in a business pursuit. Learning how to negotiate successfully makes the process enjoyable and rewarding.

Very few books on negotiation mention purchasing except as an obstacle to making a sale. Books written by lawyers reflect their training in adversarial representation and lack the mutual benefit approach required for advantageous commercial negotiation. For academics, the negotiation experience consists of studying and interviewing others, and then theorizing applications. Presented from the sales angle, negotiation consists largely of techniques calculated to increase the close ratio. All such books offer limited value to the practicing buyer – and we are all buyers!

Skill and success in negotiation can not be acquired by practice alone. Practice must be supplemented by a study of this rather loosely organized discipline. Negotiation has no well-defined rules, as in an athletic contest. Nor is it a cumulative science as mathematics, wherein algebra must precede calculus. Think of negotiation as a living, changeable art form, much as is grammar. It is exactly this amorphous character that makes the challenge of successful negotiation so interesting, satisfying, and exciting.

This book incorporates the larger scope of business practice and fosters the proper view of negotiation as the heart of the purchasing profit center. Sales pros eager to learn a consultative approach to provide measurable extra value to the customer will gain unique insights.

Since business negotiation necessarily involves contracts and law, these matters will be integrated in context. The successful practice of negotiation also encompasses the human qualities that generate such fascinating, frustrating, and confusing interpersonal webs. The human dimensions extend to verbal communication, personality styles, and into the mysterious genre of body language. It is helpful to think of each of these disciplines as tools with which to stock the negotiator's tool chest.

This book also exemplifies the concept of added value from the purchasing point of view. Ironically, negotiation expertise, although the core competency of the purchasing trade, has traditionally been the hallmark of the winning sales pros. Indeed, on the 50th anniversary of Arthur Miller's classic play, *Death of a Salesman*, a national newspapers[2] front-page story noted that the 15.5 million sales professionals in the US receive an average of 38 hours of training per year. Much of that sales training stresses presentation, communication and negotiation techniques.

On the contrary, the Institute of Supply Management, ISM (formerly The National Association of Purchasing Management, NAPM), estimates that about 30,000 purchasing professionals have earned the designation of Certified Purchasing Manager, requiring dedication to training and professional study. According to Dr. Harry Hough, president of the American Purchasing Society (APS), some 300,000 folks refer to their career designation as buyers, purchasers, materials managers or other procurement titles. This stunning disparity between the huge population of sales and miniscule number of purchasing personnel underscores a phenomenon that even the greenest buyers recognize at first glance. Every dollar saved by purchasing earns ten, twenty, or more times the profit earned by the sales dollar. Despite this fact, purchasing has traditionally not been viewed as a profit center, and, therefore, little to no attention is devoted to the essential skill of negotiation.

The value of purchasing to the success of business cannot be

---

[2] USA Today, February 9, 1999, page 1

overstated. Most upper level executives of large organizations with whom I have spoken understand intuitively that "we make money when we buy; we just collect when we sell." Consider the graphic proof shown in this chart.

Cost Breakdown	Base Sales	Sales Up 10%	Costs Down 10%
	$1,000,000	$1,100,000	$1,000,000
Material	$450,000	$495,000	$405,000
Labor	$450,000	$495,000	$405,000
TOTAL	$900,000	$990,000	$810,000
Profit	$100,000	$110,000	$190,000
Effect on Profit	Base	Up 10%	Up 90%

The contribution of purchasing to profit is enormous, dwarfing that of sales by comparison. Given that this model assumes a 10% profit, the contribution is likely understated. At 5% profitability, the contribution from purchasing would be double, or 180% that of sales. Can anyone doubt that purchasing is the most efficient profit generator in business?

Perhaps the most enjoyable by-product of the study and mastery of negotiation is the elimination of stress and aggravation that accompanies every unskilled negotiator's efforts. You will acquire a new spirit and appreciation to your pursuit, one that is reinforced and rewarded on virtually a daily basis.

Introduction

The practice of professional purchasing has lacked a definitive resource on its central competency, negotiation, until Robert Menard took up the challenge of bringing this book to the marketplace. When I set out more than 30 years ago to create the first professional purchasing society in the U.S. and the first certification for purchasing professionals, very few resources existed to help dedicated procurement pros improve business operations.

In the ensuing years, this profession has worked diligently to upgrade its knowledge base. Well known, informative books on purchasing law, supplier management, contract management techniques, and other disciplines essential to the practice of purchasing management are now on the desks of top business executives. Most businesses now recognize the enormous contribution and return on investment that purchasing makes, referring rightfully to the profit center nature of purchasing.

Many of these valuable works have contained chapters on negotiation, most all of which were valuable, albeit incomplete. This work by Robert Menard represents the first book to incorporate the principles of professional purchasing into negotiation. For instance, a central concept to procurement is the Total Cost of Ownership. Menard weaves together a seamless fabric of negotiation principles around this central concept. The book has ample examples to illustrate and reinforce the material.

It is no accident that this first book to address the specific issues of buyers in negotiation is written by a buyer, a Certified Purchasing Professional accredited by the American Purchasing Society. For example, take two topics that might otherwise be viewed as esoteric - Cost Analysis and Price Analysis. These are presented in a meaningful fashion, related to workplace challenges, and distilled to the essence of applicability.

It takes real world experience in the profession, a mastery of purchasing management principles, and a knack at expression to bring this material to life. It is not the "been there, done that" disdain of some, or the "above the fray" condescension of others that is required to produce this seminal piece, but Robert Menard's uncanny ability to seize upon his life experience and professional skill to deliver this singular work on negotiation.

Harry Hough, Ph.D., CPP

President, American Purchasing Society

Table of Contents

Chapter 1

Redefining Negotiation

The *Adversarial* View of Negotiation

Negotiation has long endured an image problem. It evokes negative emotions related to conflict, dishonesty, and stress. A popular view of negotiation holds that it is merely the evolved version of barbarian warfare, where the more powerful, better-armed and psychologically superior negotiator engages only in winner takes all brutality. The vanquished can expect scorched earth and the sacrifice of all prisoners while the victor enjoys the concubine pleasures of conquest.

Our American culture tends to generate Win-Lose results and thereby reinforce the adversarial view of any conflict, let alone negotiation. The (I) Win- (You) Lose form is by far the most popularly practiced in negotiation, and sometimes the only form with which many business executives feel comfortable.

Among the abundant examples our culture provides...

1. Consider the mystique of *Monday Night Football*. Bigger, stronger, meaner and faster are admired, if not required, commodities. In fact, for many years, the pre-game

television promo has included the electronic smashing of helmets.

2. The trite tactics of the seller trying to inflate prices and the buyer attempting to troll for an unreasonable deal accompany virtually every yard sale transaction in this country.

3. The Hollywood miser of legend foreclosing on the orphanage invites the conclusion that all is fair in negotiation.

4. The media images of bloodthirsty lawyers, mega-moguls, and ego-driven tycoons negotiating all-or-nothing deals reinforce the stereotype.

The result is a host of negative negotiation fantasies and misconceptions pervasive in business...

> *"Lying and dishonesty are expected and required."*
>
> *"I don't negotiate!" "If we can get down to the price issue now, we can save a lot of time."*
>
> *"There has to be a winner and a loser, and I know which one I'm going to be."*
>
> *"They are bigger, therefore more powerful."*
>
> *"Take it or leave it is the best policy."*
>
> *"What could I possibly have that would interest them?"*
>
> *"I can not afford to lose this deal, no matter what the cost."*
>
> *"The side with more money always wins."*
>
> *"The whole affair is too stressful."*

Due to this distortion of negotiation, many folks prefer to distance themselves from such a distasteful pursuit. Even buyers in large and sophisticated companies sometimes do not exhibit good negotiation skills. The fact is that we all negotiate, and we do it all of the time. Any time you attempt to persuade someone to a certain way of thinking, or to motivate someone else to accept a mutually beneficial proposal, or to just get something you want, you are negotiating. Yet very few business schools, corporate training programs and purchasing pros concentrate on the formal study of negotiation.

Despite these facts of business life, many of us insist that we are good negotiators. This belief may stem from isolated "victories," effective personality traits, or the tendency to pick an easy target. In seminars, I frequently ask folks how they measure their negotiation efficiency. The most common response relates to the body count – the more in their favor, the better they did. Later in the day, when we discuss rationales for Lose-Win, wherein one decides to "lose" and let the opposing party "win", their reaction is mild amazement that one could plan to lose small in the short term yet to win big in the long term. While the investment of short-term sacrifice for long-term gain is not foreign to most people, the very notion of losing a negotiation is such anathema that one resorts to winning at all costs.

The caricature of Igor from purchasing, the overworked, paper-pushing slave illustrates reality more than comedy for many unskilled Buyers. Much of the reason that Purchasing has earned this unflattering reputation relates to the lack of training and ongoing education prevalent in negotiation.

Contrast this view of the buyer with that of the seller portrayed in a front page *Wall Street Journal* article[3]. *"...new sales reps have been through 40 simulated sales calls, many of them videotaped...training sessions now include 30-second encounters in parking lots and office hallways."*

Clearly, the divide between the average practicing buyer and seller is widest in the area of training, particularly negotiation training. Let's set about narrowing that gap with a view of negotiating for success.

The *Advantageous* View of Negotiation

A better vision of negotiation has far more value to business pros. It revolves around the somewhat over used and under appreciated

---

[3] Wall Street Journal, June 13, 2003, page 1

conflict resolution strategy of Win-Win negotiation.

Certainly, many incarnations of Win-Win exist, but two underpinnings of business life remain steady.

For one, the parties to a negotiation do not want the same thing, as we will soon prove. Secondly, the reason we negotiate is that the other party has something that we want. These two simple realities provide the very basis for Advantageous Negotiations. That is, exactly because Buyer and Seller do not want the same thing, each can get what they want without denying the other side what it wants. Adding to this the fact that someone else always has what we want forces us to accept conflict as a normal and mandatory precondition for negotiation and to devise a way for the other side to get what they want in order to satisfy ourselves.

The Rules of Advantageous Negotiation

Rule 1
Negotiation requires and resolves conflict.

If the other side has what we want, conflict exists. Since effective and meaningful negotiation cannot proceed without it, conflict is good, indeed mandatory for the negotiation process to operate. No negotiation occurs if two parties agree. Consider this fruit stand sale.

> **Grocer**: *"I want 500 pounds of peaches."*
>
> **Farmer**: *"The price is $1 per pound."*
>
> **Grocer**: *"Great. Here you are."*

Agreement was instantaneous. Conflict, if it existed at all, played no role in this transaction. Therefore, negotiation, as a conflict resolution vehicle, demands that parties disagree, that conflict be the basis of the transaction. This imbedded conflict cannot be minimized. It helps to envision conflict as rain. Rain is never generally welcomed, but expected, and we appreciate it for the good that it does.

The key element here is <u>resolution</u> of conflict. One of the logical consequences of Adversarial Negotiation is the <u>inflammation</u> of conflict. The mindset of adversaries is "We have conflict here. What other issues can we fight over to get this settled all at once? (In our favor, naturally.)" Recall one of the most successful and best made war movies of all time, *Patton.* Most of us would agree that war is the quintessential embodiment of Win-Lose mentality, as well as the ultimate break down of negotiation. In a career distinguishing performance, George C. Scott, who portrayed the title character of WW II fame, utters the consummate conflict-inflammation lines about the Russians. "We'll have to fight the sons of bitches sometime, so let's do it here and now when we have the men, equipment and resources". Patton was not a big believer in negotiation, perhaps, but a handy guy to have around when negotiations fail. In business, thankfully, we usually do not have to take quite such drastic action as did General Patton.

Rule 2
Each party to the transaction does not want the same thing.

Now let's add to the mix the fact that each party wants something other than what the other side wants. In the Buy-Sell setting, what does the Seller want from the Buyer? In one word, the seller wants the order, the sale, the profit, or, shall we say, the MONEY. Contrast this to the one word answer to what the Buyer wants from the Seller; the goods, the services, the STUFF. The Buyer already has the money and wants the stuff. The Seller already has the stuff and wants the money. This business reality makes perfect capitalistic and logical sense. Yet, it often does not seem clear to many parties involved in a transaction. Further, for the Seller, the money need not be in the form of cash payment. It may take the form of future sales commitments, or increased market share or motivations of which the Buyer has no knowledge. For the Buyer, the stuff may be worth more or less, depending upon certain values. For instance, the latest microprocessor may be worth more as a marketing tool than as a piece of hardware to an assembler or Value Added Reseller (VAR) in the computer industry. These added dimensions to the Buy-Sell setting provide many opportunities for both Buyer and Seller to obtain what they need to win.

Let's return to the fruit stand example, keeping in mind that the parties want different results from the negotiation.

Grocer: *"I want 500 pounds of peaches."*

Farmer: *"The price is $1 per pound."*

Grocer: *"Does that price include delivery? What is the freshness and species of these peaches? Do you stock the shelves?"*

Farmer: *"Well, in that case the price depends on your specifications."*

Rule 3
Negotiation is a Process, Not an Event.

It is very helpful to visualize negotiation as a continuous process, and not an isolated event. The ancient Chinese adage states that the longest journey begins with but the first step. Yet, we are conditioned to the seductive suggestion that one "goes into negotiations" for a fixed period. For example, every year, school committees and teachers' unions around the country wrestle with contract renewal matters. Are the weeks immediately preceding school resumption a preordained and sacred time reserved for these negotiations? Americans are familiar with the annual spring ritual of baseball players who posture for fan sympathy, releasing threatening press releases all winter long before finally signing at the deadline. Many buyers consider negotiation an interruption, a tension-filled, face-to-face speed bump. We then file away our notes, put the order-ship-bill-pay cycle on autopilot, and then forget about the supplier until the next problem arises.

The process begins with supplier sourcing and continues in a variety of manifestations throughout the course of the relationship. The process encompasses an exchange of one thing for another, usually money for stuff, as we have seen. The reason that negotiation is thought of as an event and not a process is the equating of face-to-face meetings with the "act" of negotiation. As is true with most of life's permanent endeavors, preparation constitutes about 80% of the effort. The face-to-face encounters will average only a fraction of the total time involved, say 5 to 10 percent. The majority of the negotiation work will be invested in these strategic pursuits:

1. Investigation, design and implementation of **Supplier Certification** (sometimes called a Qualification) program

2. Application and periodic review of a **Supplier Evaluation** program

3. Management of Supplier using Performance Metrics

4. Visits to the Supplier's facilities

5. Analysis of financial statements

6. Analysis of Price and Cost structures

7. Development of new suppliers, systems, products and services

These seven pursuits require substantial upfront investments of time and energy of the professional buyer. The natural question that arises is the justification for this effort. What is the payoff to be expected of all this time-consuming, labor-intensive and expensive activity? Among the most tangible and useful benefits are:

✓ Verifiable data based objective criteria needed to make rational business decisions

✓ Systematic information for

- Rewarding supplier behavior

- Justifying purchasing decisions

- Improving supplier performance

✓ Reduction of problems with suppliers before they occur

✓ Elimination of inappropriate or inadequate suppliers

✓ A payoff in savings of time, cost and needless aggravation for the Purchasing negotiator

✓ Dollars-and-numbers criteria for improving the relationship between buyer and seller

Everyone talks about Win-Win Negotiation, and most have their own definition. However defined (we will define ours in Chapter 5), Win-Win negotiation exists because of the synthesis of Rules 1, 2, and 3 above. The Rules combine to offer occasions for Win-Win outcomes that would not be possible under the adversarial regime of negotiation. The inherent conflict brings parties together in an effort to make an exchange. The deal revolves around the reality that one party has something that the other party wants. Thorough application of the process generates a continuous stream of well researched, mutually beneficial opportunities that enjoy high probabilities for success.

Workplace example:

A case study is helpful in putting these ideas into practical perspective. Let's take a moment to consider how Advantageous Negotiation turns the tide in business.

History: In the 1970's, the US automotive industry stared down the barrel of extinction. Total Quality Management (TQM) was not warmly embraced in the US during the post WW II economic boom years. The theory proved beneficial and flourished in Japan, however, contributing to that country's economic rise from the wartime ash heap to a reinvigorated industrial giant 25 years after Nagasaki. Japanese automobile manufacturers implemented the principles of TQM and challenged the Big 3 by the early 80's. US-made autos lagged behind Japanese models in quality and resale value. Earnings of US automakers plummeted as unemployment rose and market share dropped. Chrysler faced bankruptcy.

These threats to survival spurred the US auto industry to adopt mandates of TQM, in fact improving upon them. Ford ads with a catchy jingle proclaimed *"Quality is job 1"*. Not only did the US auto makers improve their quality, but institutionalized it. The Big 3 formulated Quality Standards (QS) 9000 that simulated ISO methodology but fostered more rigorous application to the auto industry.

Conclusion: As is characteristically true of negotiation, one can reach the same outcome via many different routes. Nevertheless, the economic compulsion to reduce costs is the prime mover in business. The auto makers, their suppliers, and the unions had to confront a major watershed issue: How will the benefits of cost reduction, and therefore continued market viability be shared and the implementation effected?

The auto makers needed to first adopt a new culture and then to prevail on its suppliers and the unions of the wisdom of its perspective. This task became a long term effort to communicate and participate in a major business revolution. **In business, this communication and participation takes the form of negotiation.**

The rules of Advantageous Negotiation apply to our workplace example in this fashion:

Rule 1
Conflict could hardly be more profound than the verge of extinction or bankruptcy. The inherent conflict between the auto makers and their suppliers took many forms. Should the suppliers bail out in favor of new and different customers and industries? What would be the expected return for the sacrifice to be made by the suppliers? Would the US auto makers be able to fend off the superiority gained by the foreign competitors?

Rule 2
The Big 3 auto makers may have wanted many things in which the suppliers had no great interest. For instance, continued viability was certainly an issue for Chrysler but probably much less so to many of its suppliers.

Rule 3
The process took place over many years and continues to this day.

A question that arises in our business pursuits is, "If Adversarial Negotiation is so powerful and effective, why and how does it fail?" The next logical question is, "What happens when our negotiation efforts fail?" A famous quote helps to gain perspective. In the turbulent, Cold War 60's, President Kennedy said in an important speech, "Let us never negotiate from fear, but let us never fear to negotiate". The moral applies to the business world. Running for one's lawyers guarantees a reallocation of wealth, usually from the client's pocket to that of the lawyer's. The proper time for one's lawyers is <u>before</u> a problem arises.

Robert Ringer's *"Winning Through Intimidation"* (Ringer, 1973) pointed out that for any business venture to succeed, it must win in the jungle. To paraphrase his meaning, negotiation beats litigation. Lawyers earn many times their fees for clients when we put their advice to work before the fact. A competent lawyer's counsel will be of inestimable value when we do not wait for the problem to happen before we call. When we have to fund an enormous expenditure to grind the sluggish wheels of justice, the importance of negotiation becomes an apparent and very attractive alternative.

Consider the maxim found posted in many lawyers' offices – Talk is cheap until you talk to a lawyer! As a matter of business practice, it is the failure of negotiation that invites legal remedies. Court action can be very time-consuming, nearly always costs far in excess of a negotiated solution, and usually creates a less-than-satisfying or pleasant experience for the litigants. Putting aside the expense for the moment, the aura of negative energy can paralyze one's effectiveness. A single tribulation will convince most skeptics that there is no such thing as the justice system, which is why it is called the legal system. The system wastes countless hours in the discovery stage, searching for and producing documents, answering pointless, repetitive interrogatories, enduring endless hours of nasty depositions…

And what happens back at the office? Does the Purchasing Fairy dash in and clean up the work on your desk? Add to all of this aggravation the loss of opportunities and time. The sum becomes more than most of us are willing to pay. In Chapter 8 we will account for the aspects of law that control purchasing behavior.

Bear in mind that negotiation resolves conflicts and disputes. Negotiations can break down for a variety of causes attributable to one or both parties. Among these are five chief reasons:

1. Bad faith, including incompetent or unauthorized negotiators

2. Fraud, or other illegal actions

3. Stubbornness or ignorance

4. Inability or lack of willingness to negotiate

5. Inadequate negotiation skills.

We will acquire tools throughout this book to eliminate these problems as we strengthen our negotiation skills. The goal is to always be in a position to be successful through negotiation. It is always the first and preferred course of action. We stress that in the legal and the business arenas, negotiation is considered a form of dispute resolution alternative to litigation - and it is always the better alternative.

Summary

Adversarial Negotiation begins at an argument over price and heads downhill. It is a "me-versus-you" natural mode of conflict resolution that gives little consideration to the other party.

Advantageous Negotiation advances the proposition that each side can attain what they want. To do so requires the observance of three rules:

1. Negotiation requires and resolves conflict.
2. The parties do not want the same thing.
3. Negotiation is a process, not an event.

> *"Beatings will continue until morale improves."*
> Advice on a US Army boot camp barracks wall

Chapter 2

Total Cost of Ownership

Total Cost of Ownership (TCO) is the single most important principle in all of supply chain management. The TCO concept has evolved from near cult status to preeminence. TCO quantifies and measures costs. The principle of TCO has impacted Advantageous Negotiations by expanding the narrow confines of "Price Only" negotiation to a vast field of opportunities for attaining Win-Win results. Anyone can get a lower price. The object of good business is to attain the lowest TCO.

In professional purchasing, we can reduce the essence of everything we do to a single word – **Cost**. Any discipline (logistics, inventory, purchasing, etc.) falling under the umbrella of Supply Chain Management can be interpreted and expressed in terms of Cost. The relationship between Cost and Value is that the Best Value means the lowest TCO.

Many of us carelessly confuse the concepts of price and cost, using them interchangeably. To define them simply, price is the money coming in, cost is the money going out and profit is the difference. For this reason, cost management is crucial to business success. For two companies selling at competitive prices, the higher cost company realizes lower profits. Basic economics show that high costs are bad for business.

Well, what exactly is TCO, how is it measured and how does it affect negotiation? First, let us identify the four elements of cost and demonstrate the impact of each on TCO.

The four elements of cost are:

Quality, **S**ervice, **D**elivery, and **P**rice (**QSDP**)

TCO = the sum of the cost elements

or

TCO = Quality + Service + Delivery + Price

Several facts about TCO must be recognized and appreciated to conduct an effective negotiation:

1. Each element of QSDP has an impact on the TCO.

2. The importance of each element varies with the product or service being purchased.

3. The relative weight of each element depends upon our assessment of the TCO impact on our business.

4. The identity and weight of each element is an ongoing part of the continuous negotiation process.

Price is not only different from cost, but is merely one element of cost. The impact of the other elements usually dwarfs the impact of price. Let's take the example of the sorry used-car purchase.

"Have I got a deal for you," intones the stereotypical used-car salesman dressed in plaids and stripes. He probably means a deal on the price, certainly not the cost. By the time you pay for the new transmission, replace the leaky valves, and meet all the inspection standards, the total cost encourages you to reconsider the wisdom of alternative methods of transportation.

In order to negotiate effectively, buyers and sellers must understand and evaluate the cost impact of each of the four elements of QSDP. In fact, our negotiation plan, which we will map out in the next chapter, will be built around the TCO.

Quality

Given the emphasis on quality in business today, is Quality always the most important element of cost? Often it is. Take the case of medical goods, such as heart valves for cardiac surgery. Assume further that you are the patient, and the dominance that Quality enjoys in the TCO calculation becomes quite obvious.

Service

Service tends to be more important in certain acquisitions, such as high tech goods and services, and in labor contract agreements. If the air conditioning goes down in your Alabama facility in July, you want someone, anyone, to arrive on site with 15 minutes. Even an apprentice can check the gauges, fluid levels, belts, breakers, etc., while awaiting the arrival of the rest of the service crew.

Delivery

Suppose, though, that you operate a hydraulic press line where one pump powers twenty presses, and that pump fails. Do you then want a pump, any pump? Would you take a temporary replacement of too high or low a pressure until the correct pump comes in? More than likely, yes, "Just get me a pump! I'll reduce the pressure or eliminate several presses." In this case, Delivery far exceeds the impact of the other costs.

Price

Now we arrive at Price. Many times, Price is clearly and justifiably the most important element of cost. Small expense items are good examples. Take the purchase of No. 2 pencils, for example. Quality is probably not a very big issue. They are plentiful, so Delivery falls out of the equation, and what Service is involved with a pencil? So by default, the most important element is Price.

If we are constantly focusing on Price alone, we are not recognizing the impact of TCO. *Purchasing* Magazine[4] reported that 69% of businesses purchasing departments have a system (formal or informal) for rating supplier performance, and Price is rated highest by only 12 percent! Even the most casual buyer has seen the mirage of a low price evaporate into a costly burn. Every buyer will deliberately, or unconsciously, pay more if that Price premium buys a lower TCO.

---

[4] Purchasing Magazine, July 15, 1999, page 74, Cahners Publishing

The relative importance of the cost elements allows each party in the negotiation to achieve its goals. Advantageous Negotiations proceed from the principles of TCO. Here is a simple example. A buyer of Maintenance Repair and Operations (MRO) may be more concerned with having parts on hand at the supplier (Delivery) than with the Price. Downtime costs and lost income caused by not having a low-value replacement part available would far outweigh any Price advantage from the seller's competitor and thus is justifiably worth a higher price. The buyer attains its objective of availability and lower TCO and the supplier earns a price premium. Economically, it may cost the supplier more to warehouse the customer's parts, and therefore a slightly higher price is cost-defensible. The supplier may understandably try to leverage that advantage into the highest supportable price. It the price gets too high, the buyer will recalculate its TCO.

Each of the QSDP elements can be further broken down into sub-elements. This exercise is a wise investment for three reasons:

1. They will create the basis for a Supplier Certification program.

2. They will be assigned metrics to measure the supplier's performance in your Supplier Evaluation program.

3. They form the foundation of your negotiation plan that we will set forth in Chapter 3.

Let's see how we could break down the elements of QSDP as they relate to a purchase negotiation.

Quality has as many manifestations as we deem are important to the specific purchase. In manufacturing, non-conforming material must be rejected, adding costs to the process. In the food industry, freshness and shelf life of perishables may be a major criterion. The same rationale is true for the other cost elements. Delivery may include transportation and storage costs, Service could include response time and technical personnel, and Price might include discounts and payment terms. These are just a few possible rationales. Each has an impact on the overall cost, and we must evaluate how significant that impact is. In other words, we must know our costs. That is an eminently logical and mandatory piece of advice, but it is not at all obvious, based on the performance of many negotiators.

The following are just a few common sub-elements of QSDP. Adapt yours to suit the particular purchase.

Quality

Rejection percentage
Shelf life Reliability
Useful life
Maintenance, repair and operating costs
Salvage value or trade-in
Quality Control/Quality Assurance
Off-site testing/certification
Remedy policy Scrap rate

Delivery

Transportation
Storage
Stocking programs
On-time percentage
Packaging and/or put up
Drop shipments

Service

Response time
On-site representation
Technical competence
Electronic capability
Advertising
Tooling
Exclusivity
Research and development
Warranties

Price

Payment terms
Price-change terms
Minimum-order quantities and charges
Discounts
Lease versus buy and lease-buy options
Ownership of licenses, patents, etc.

Many more can and should be added, depending upon your

situation. These are the issues upon which we form our negotiation plan. We will build the plan and concession strategy around these quantifiable and measurable elements of cost so as to achieve the lowest TCO.

Let's apply this principle to a purchase that we can reference as we move through our negotiation planning. If we were to buy concrete railroad ties, here is how we might rate QSDP.

Concrete Railroad Ties

1. **Q**uality
2. **D**elivery
3. **P**rice
4. **S**ervice

We chose this order because we've determined that the time between replacements (useful life) was most critical to us in terms of overall cost. The longer the time between replacements, the more the rail lines remain unblocked and available for revenue producing use by customers. So **Quality** ranked uppermost.

Delivery was next the most important cost. Concrete ties are not as plentiful as wood ties are around most of the nation, so provision will need to be made in the negotiation for ensuring availability.

Price came next, and Service last. **Service** has virtually no cost component in ties because the Quality element dominates. With high-enough Quality, we won't need Service and its associated costs. Price, therefore, came in third by default.

All we need to do now is break out some sub-elements of QSDP and we are done for the moment. For Quality, we could use rejection percentage, useful life, scrap rate, and remedy policies. Delivery costs could include transportation and storage. Service might encompass technical competence or electronic capability, while Price could take in payment and price change terms. We summarize these results in the following table.

Concrete Railroad Ties

Quality
- Rejection percentage
- Useful life
- Scrap rate
- Remedy policy

Delivery
- Transportation
- Storage

Price
- Payment terms
- Price change terms

Service
- Technical competence
- Electronic capability

This is exactly the type of exercise we must complete for every significant purchase. Once we do it, change is unlikely unless underlying cost structures for our business change, so this is well worth the effort.

The most important element of cost will have the greatest number of sub-elements. This pattern is characteristic of the TCO model and makes eminent sense. If it is more important, it should have more manifestations.

Now we arrive at interesting crossroads. We have defined the TCO concept and found that price is actually an element of cost. Yet, the vast preponderance of business negotiations revolves around either cost or price, usually price. Buyers and sellers negotiate and argue over price and cost as if these were two vague, disconnected, yet somehow philosophical sources of conflict. Which came first, the price or the cost? This is a good point to pause and examine the very nature of negotiation as it relates to and incorporates price and cost.

We can no more settle the price and cost question than we can its chicken and egg counterpart. Let's see how they are related because Price Analysis is the logical precursor to its close cousin, Cost Analysis.

Price Analysis

Haven't you wondered from time to time about how Price is established? Do they come down from the mount on stone tablets? Some years ago, while living on the East Coast, I was constantly traveling coast to coast doing seminars and speeches on purchasing and negotiation. During a particular two-week stretch in May, I was working in California so I stayed for the intervening weekend. On the shuttle flight from Los Angeles to San Francisco, I bought both the LA and San Francisco newspapers. Each had a dozen or more pages of classified ads for sales openings, as will any major metropolitan Sunday paper. Having always been intrigued by the differences in sales-think versus purchasing-think, the ads for 'Sales Analyst," "Pricing Strategists," and "Marketing Specialists" attracted my attention. The one or two pages of ads for purchasing positions never list such creative titles, just hierarchal references such as buyer, Director of Purchasing or Materials Manager. These positions lack the intrigue of, say, "Pricing Strategist."

The allure of such curious titles notwithstanding, the shroud of mystery in establishing a Price seems rather transparent. Ask ten people how it is done, and nine will say that the supplier takes its cost and adds a percentage for profit. That percentage may vary, depending on market conditions and other factors, but basically Price is considered to be figured as some multiple of cost. We will use 10% for simplicity. If the supplier's cost is $0.90-$0.91 per unit, then a 10 % profit means that the Price should be $1.00 each.

There is a good reason why buyers have been trained by sellers to think in this cost-plus-percentage mode. The seller has a ready answer to the buyer's price reduction demand. *"Look"*, the salesman can offer flatly while turning his empty hip pocket inside out, *"I cannot possibly reduce the Price because I have so little on it now!"*

The origins and evolution of prices are usually not quite as simple as the common cost-plus-percentage chestnut might suggest. One of our first tasks in negotiation is to ascertain how Price is established. This process is called Price Analysis. The following list contains some of the most popular strategies for pricing products or services. We will examine each for their negotiation value.

Popular Pricing Strategies

- ➤ Cost plus a mark-up
- ➤ Survival
- ➤ Target
- ➤ Traffic
- ➤ Revenue Management
- ➤ Yield Management
- ➤ Perceived Value

<u>Cost plus a mark-up</u>

This is by far the most predominant of pricing strategies. Many products and services have been around for a while and may have lost unique character. Two common reasons are the expiration of patents and the emergence of competitive and/ or replacement products and/or services. Any mature product or service in a mature market probably falls into this category. Portland cement, high-heel shoes, thermo-set plastics, laundry detergent and automobiles are common examples. In these markets, the bloom has long fallen from the rose. In other words, these products and services no longer lend themselves to exotic forms of pricing. The buyer has extensive experience and knowledge of the product and market and thus the range of Price is relatively constrained.

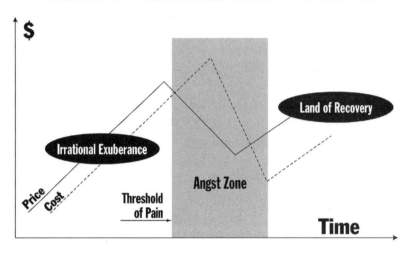

Figure 2-1

"Mature" Markets and Products

Figure 2-1 shows the pricing cycle as products mature in their markets. Rapid price growth occurs early on, usually accompanied by loose cost control. This area is labeled **Irrational Exuberance**.

At some time in the product cycle, competition emerges, causing extreme unease in the seller as revenues tied to an artificially high price begin a steep plunge. This is the **Angst Zone**. Symptoms include a dizzy feeling of "how could this happen?" followed by the conclusion that "we must cut costs to survive." Since those costs have not been managed with care, costs exceed revenues as far as the eye can see.

Then, as equilibrium sets in, the price truly becomes related to the cost as margins become regular and costs are managed better. This is the **Land of Recovery** where business settles into a comfortable cost-plus-percentage mode.

For negotiation's sake, buyers must know where they and the suppliers are in this cycle. Anyone who bought high-tech stocks in the late 90's and suffered through the painful stock crash knows just how important this is. The shares of dot-com, which mostly became dot-gones, brought huge prices in the early stages. Many had no Price/Earnings multiples because they had never made money, ever, yet the stock prices commanded huge, irrational premiums. During the **Angst Zone**, millions of investors lost trillions in market value. As **Recovery** set in, those caught up in the **Irrational Exuberance** have become more conservative and suspicious of prices.

Survival

Next on the Price Analysis list is an item with which we are probably familiar -survival. This pricing strategy results directly from competition, usually in the form of a lower-cost supplier, in the market place. A good example is Southwest Airlines. They have made low-cost, reliable air transportation their hallmark. No-frills, usually timely, and certainly a challenge to their competitors, they caused huge ripples in the market when they expanded nationally in the 90's. Southwest's low-cost structure translated directly to lower priced air fares, which upset the hub and spoke systems of competitors in the air transportation system. Fare prices of the larger national competitors fell to meet Southwest's market challenge and had no relationship to the costs. Rather it was a matter of survival. If Southwest could capture market share with low prices, then they might be able to capitalize on connecting flights and that would seriously threaten survival of the hub and spoke airlines. This pricing strategy can be dangerous for the buyer as well as the seller, particularly if the price is driven too low. The supplier might not stay in business, and the buyer might incur Robinson-Patman problems in the purchase of goods. We will examine this and other legal influences in Chapter 8.

Target

Target pricing might not be obvious to the buyer at all. The buyer may even think that it is something she has done to deserve preferential treatment. More likely, the pricing depends upon a strategic decision by the supplier to capture a market segment.

Suppose that you are a school book publisher. Your ideal customer is a school district that buys 1,000,000 books annually. Assume further that you want to neutralize certain aggressive competitors who have been nipping on your heels, cutting into your customer base.

An effective strategy for corralling the best prospects while icing competitors may be to target those customers who appeal to your strengths, produce the greatest return for the least investment (cost), and who can bring you other customers as a result of your sales initiatives. Meanwhile, you are mining every opportunity to generate future business from similar customers. You approach other prospects with verifiable success stories of how the target customer has been well served and thus should join up as another preferred customer. The motivation could be customer size, industry, location or other factors. The point to keep in mind is that this is a common pricing strategy and one that needs to be identified by the buyer as a negotiation technique.

Traffic

We have all heard about 'what the traffic will bear' as a pricing strategy. It usually means that the seller is gambling that the market is good therefore the law of supply and demand swings in its favor. This strategy is merely a variation of the cost-plus-percentage mode as a 'normal' mark-up is augmented by a premium to reflect market conditions. The science of economics, as with so many factors in negotiation, may not tell the whole story. Might the supplier have other motivations? What about the salesperson who stands to win the trip to Hawaii if she makes this next sale to you? Supply and demand, margin, and even pride all fade in the glow of making this sale.

At home, we once had a door-to-door newspaper subscription hawker who offered coupons at a local restaurant if we would subscribe to the paper. It did not matter if we actually paid for the paper after the free test period as long as he got credit for writing the subscription. Doubtful of the explanation, I phoned the paper. A helpful but naïve fellow explained that the two local competing papers were being audited. Higher subscription counts bring higher advertising rates. So the subscription Price, whether I continued or not, had nothing to do with the paper's costs. Sometimes, this *Traffic* strategy is not all that it seems.

Revenue Management

This one shines with sophistication. Its very name reeks with confusion, much like lawyers conversing in Latin terms or physicians speaking in advanced chemistry. As one famous, if quirky, American politico once observed, though, things are more practical where the rubber meets the road. We will heed Ross Perot's advice and reduce this strategy to familiar terms. Here is how it works in the case of the airlines.

Under certain advance-purchase conditions, most airlines offer super saver fares. Usually, it is the personal traveler who enjoys the schedule flexibility to take advantage of these deeply discounted fares. The super saver fare is often just a fraction of the full-price coach ticket.

Say that $300 is a reasonable fare for a coast-to-coast, roundtrip super saver fare. The business traveler suffers the disadvantage of minimum advance planning. For instance, I once had a client call on my cell phone while I was on the way to the airport and drastically change our whole itinerary. With less than an hour before the flight and in a hot sweaty hurry, I purchased a round-trip, coast-to-coast coach ticket for about $3,000. Can you imagine the conversation I had with the passenger who sat right beside me? She purchased her ticket for $300. I paid ten times that amount. Thankfully, she never asked me if my seat was really ten times better. I also never gave her my business card with the inscription "America's Best Purchasing and Negotiation Speaker, Trainer, and Consultant."

Yet, the airlines make eloquent and in part logical arguments that this pricing strategy is not only sensible, but required.

Otherwise, too many passengers would show up for some flights and not enough for others. Therefore, this strategy, which effectively penalizes the businesses traveler, was actually maintaining order where chaos would otherwise rule. You be the judge. The important point to recognize is that an opportunity exists to clarify the interests of buyer and seller. Large travel brokers smooth out these price swings in fares by purchasing blocks of seats and reselling them. Consolidators peddle seats online, to tour agencies, or to the public, thereby filling the gap between the super saver and at-the-gate price. How does your supplier price its product or service? Is it by some mysterious method such as Revenue Management? If so, it needs to be addressed in negotiations.

Yield Management

This strategy is completely counter-intuitive and seems to defy logic. The hospitality industry is a leading case in point here. Suppose you operated a 300-room hotel, and one night you have a 50% vacancy. What would be better for business: To demand the 'rack" rate (usually the highest posted rate) because you need the revenue, or to offer the lowest rate possible just to get butts in the beds? The answer is to give the deepest discounts when the occupancy is the lowest, and demand the rack rate when the occupancy is highest. I learned about this strategy the hard way. One early November weekend, I attended a meeting at a New York airport hotel. Air traffic was slow in advance of the madcap Thanksgiving Day holiday, so the hotel had many available rooms. Upon check-in, I asked the clerk about the room rates. Bear in mind that I had pre-registered at the 'convention rate' of $150. She told me that I could have a room in the convention wing for $135 or in the remote wing for $115. Curious, I inquired about the distinction. Without further ado, she offered me a room in the convention wing at the $115 rate. So much for Yield Management, I concluded.

Five months later, I was at the same airport again. My father and brothers, who lived across the US landscape, were all to meet in Miami to catch a flight to Costa Rica for a four day fishing retreat. Soon after I arrived for my connecting flight, a rogue Nor'easter blizzard blew in from New England, and all flights were cancelled. The entire airport was shutdown at 3 p.m. Being a smart fellow and experienced traveler, I immediately hopped the taxi to the same hotel I knew from the meeting the previous fall. Upon arrival, I suffered the indignity of long lines, impudent amateur travelers, and general unpleasantness.

At the check-in desk, realizing the situation, and being the realistic purchasing and negotiation pro, I graciously offered to pay the full price rack rate. To my chagrin, the clerk guffawed, pointing out to my obvious hick nature that everyone was paying rack rate plus a "weather premium," unless they were a platinum level customer or had US military clearance. Being neither, I squeaked my willingness to fork over about three times what I had paid for the same room just five months earlier. As they say in Texas, "Some times you make 8, sometimes you hit dirt."

Perceived Value

This one is my favorite and a clever, effective reflection of human nature. Here, the product is so good, has such great rewards, that you don't even ask the price. The one word, quintessential example of all time is Viagra. Who knows the price, and who cares?

Perceived value has applications beyond pharmaceuticals today. The telecommunications world has many fine examples in the wireless phone and Internet connection services. Here is how it originated.

In the mid 70's, Tagamet was the leading ulcer medication. Tagamet's success attracted competitors. Soon after, Zantac appeared on the market. Both products served the same purpose and appealed to the same customer base. The following table summarizes the performance of the competing drugs in terms of cost.

Perceived Value

Cost	Tagamet	Zantac
Quality (comparative) ▪ Interaction ▪ Side effects ▪ Dosage schedule	More More Worse More Favorable	Less Fewer Better Less Favorable
Service	Equal	Equal
Delivery	Equal	Equal
Price	(Higher Costs) **Lower Price**	(Lower Costs) **Higher Price**

This is an interesting study for a buyer. Zantac had to find a way to knock off the king of the hill, Tagamet. The advantage of better quality and lower production costs suggested adoption of the time-tested "better mousetrap" theory. That is, introduce Zantac at a lower price in order to capture market share.

That is not what some very clever execs did, however. Instead, Zantac chose to trumpet its 'Perceived Value' of fewer drug interactions, fewer side affects and better dosage schedule. Even though both drugs accomplished the same job, the greater perceived value of Zantac, reinforced through advertising, could be translated to increased price. That is exactly what happened as Zantac was brought to market at a price premium over Tagamet. Within two years, Zantac was the best selling drug on the planet.

Frequently, new product rollouts or high-tech services come to market on this pricing strategy. Voice mail provided by telephone companies is an example of a high-priced but low-cost service justified by perceived value. This is not to say that the product or service does not have actual value. On the contrary, we want to establish a basis for negotiation. We are interested at least as much in a product's cost as we are in its price.

We can summarize the myth of Price and Cost connection in the adage of the **Price/Cost Myth**, which says, "Price is related to Cost." Make anyone who says that prove it. As Ronald Reagan liked to say, "Trust, but cut the cards." This should be part of every negotiation. Whenever someone says, "Higher Price means greater value," or "You get what you pay for," think of mandatory Price Analysis.

Cost Analysis

Well, how do we make them prove it? We do so by calling upon Price Analysis's close cousin called Cost Analysis. Cost Analysis is the scrutiny given to the quantifiable and measurable breakdown of the supplier's costs that constitute its product or service.

Getting a cost breakdown is easier said than done. It depends upon how we do business. If as a buyer we own a deserved reputation for holding price auctions, divulging sensitive or confidential information to our suppliers' competitors, and otherwise violating ethics and possibly laws, of course the supplier will not trust us. To cut the cards, we have our lawyer prepare confidentiality agreements that specify non-disclosure, non-compete or whatever other covenants we as a buyer and our supplier deem important. The supplier would be either devious or foolish to trust us if we have proven that we are not worthy. Isn't our goal to attain the lowest TCO, not to lie, cheat and steal for a lower price? There is no compromise here. As people whose moral values you admire have long shown by their actions, the honest and honorable approach is the best

Cost Analysis is the single most important tool in negotiation. It brings about principled business based upon dollars-and-numbers, which is what capitalism, is all about.

The fact that both sides stand to gain is added inducement to pursue negotiation with a passion. Let's examine a few instances of how it works and its enormous influence on negotiations.

The next table presents a simple cost breakdown. This one happens to be for a telecommunications cable, but the same principle applies to medical tubing, auto parts, service level agreements, virtually every purchase. The three cost components here are Material, Production and Mark-up (overhead and profit). Material and Production are further broken down into their major constituents and subtotaled for ease of comparison. It is helpful to train ourselves to think of everything we do in cost management as represented by dollars-and-numbers. This table does that in an easily understandable fashion.

Telecommunications Cable at $2.00/linear ft			
Raw Material	Copper	40 %	$0.80
	Polyester	5 %	$0.10
	PVC	15 %	$0.30
	Subtotal	**60 %**	**$1.20**
Production	Labor	10 %	$0.20
	Indirect	10 %	$0.20
	Subcontract	10 %	$0.20
	Subtotal	**30%**	**$0.60**
Markup	**Subtotal**	**10 %**	**$0.20**
Totals		**100%**	**$2.00**

Let's scrutinize this cost breakdown. At a glance, we see that the copper tinsel comprises the greatest single cost element in this purchase. Copper therefore has the greatest impact on the cost. If we are looking at cost management, this is the first place to go because it holds the greatest reduction potential. As negotiating pros, we must educate ourselves to our suppliers' costs of the materials or services that go into what we buy. Since cost analysis is the root of all negotiation, we cannot know too much about costs.

Copper is a commodity that fluctuates daily in price. Base and precious metals, plastics, computer components, paper and paper products, fuels, and many other commodities are traded at exchanges that establish daily prices. The London Metals Exchange and the Chicago Mercantile Exchange are among the two most famous in the Western world for metals.

A client of mine was in the telecommunications hardware business. They had been buying cable assemblies over a six year period from the same supplier. During that time, the price of copper went from about $1.20 a pound in the late 80s to about half that by the mid 90s. The prices of the lesser components had not moved appreciably up or down during the same time frame.

In 1995, they engaged my services on a shared cost savings contract to dig up and fix areas of runaway cost. One of my first moves was to sort transactions by part number, history and activity. This is a good way to find where the bodies are buried. The previous table summarizes my findings. When I approached the manager about this situation, I asked how it was possible that we had been buying this cable for 6 years at the same $2.00/linear foot (lf.). He thought about it for a second and then replied, "Well, that supplier must manage its costs well."

Horse hockey, you might say, and so did I. On the basis of Cost Analysis, we had been overcharged from the first time the price fell significantly below the starting price of $1.20/ pound. We had found the enemy and it was us. The supplier, of course, was not totally innocent. He was fearful of waking us up by changing the price and ending the party that was going on in his favor with no sign of stopping. Such is the common result of adversarial-based business relationships.

As part of our ongoing negotiation process, we must acquaint and update ourselves with the cost structure dominating our supplier's raw materials and other costs. If that reasoning is insufficient, another reason to do so is the price-increase negotiation.

Assume that you buy corrugated containers from a converter. The converter buys liner board from paper mills, die-cuts it, folds it, slaps your logo on it, straps the pallets and ships it off to you. Being an exponent of the Cost religion, you have created simple Cost Analysis model for this supplier that looks like the chart below. For simplicity, the corrugated containers here carry a price of $2.00 each.

Costs of Corrugated Paper Containers			20%Price Increase
Liner Board	50 %	$1.00	$0.20
Production	40 %	$0.80	**$0.00**
Markup	10 %	$0.20	**$0.00**
Total	**100%**	**$2.00**	**$0.00**

The converter gets a price increase notice from the mill saying that the price of corrugated paper is rising 20%. The converter in turn sends you a price-increase notice saying, "The paper mill has increased the price of paper by 20%. Ergo, we regret that we are forced to raise the price we charge you by 20%!" The supplier is now demanding a 20% price premium or $0.40 more per unit to a new price of $2.40.

By applying Cost Analysis, we can immediately answer the question, "What is wrong with this picture?" The liner board is only 50% of the price. Therefore, the 20% price increase applies only to the $1.00 raw material cost component. Twenty percent of $1.00 is $0.20, or half of what the supplier was requesting. This stunt is so old that the first time it was used, the Dead Sea wasn't even sick yet.

Need more justification? How about when the price goes down? When prices of major components of the suppliers' products or services go down, when you get to the office in the morning, is your voice mail box stuffed, no longer accepting messages, because your suppliers have been calling all night saying, "We are forced to reduce the prices we charged you because our costs are less!" The next time that happens will be the first time.

A professional negotiator proactively stays on top of this situation. Where do you get information on prices? Dozens of sources are available; *The Wall Street Journal* and industry publications such as *Chemical Market Reporter*, and *American Metals Market* are but three. One good overall reference to have on hand for many reasons is *Purchasing* Magazine. It carries a regular feature called Transaction Prices. You will find current and past prices of several dozen popular commodities. Keeping track of trends is an important part of negotiation planning.

Summary

Total Cost of Ownership (TCO) is the single most important principle in all of supply chain management. Purchasing Management is Cost management. The Best Value is the lowest TCO. TCO is the sum of the elements of cost, Quality, Service, Delivery, and Price (QSDP).

Each element of QSDP can be broken down into sub-elements. We must evaluate the relative weight of each element of QSDP so that we strive to keep TCO at a minimum. To do so requires the use of two related tools, Price Analysis and its close cousin Cost Analysis, the single most important tool in negotiation.

Price Analysis is the process by which the strategy of establishing Price is learned. Cost Analysis is the scrutiny given to quantifiable and measurable breakdown of the supplier's costs that constitute its product or service. Cost Analysis brings about principled business based upon dollars-and-numbers.

Consider adopting this mission statement:

Obtain the lowest Total Cost of Ownership

- ➢ Identify, quantify and evaluate the costs of QSDP.
- ➢ Calculate the TCO.
- ➢ Negotiate an effective cost resolution.

Chapter 3

Preparing for Negotiation I

How does one prepare for negotiation other than thinking about it a lot, making some notes, and practicing at role playing? These measures are necessary but not sufficient. Preparations continue constantly in the form of learning as much as possible about the suppliers, the products or services and the markets. The cycle of learning, execution and follow-up never ends.

Very few men and women whom I have met in business invest the effort in a written negotiation plan. Maybe this failing is due to bravado. "Hey, I know what I'm doing," goes the refrain. Well, we might also know that we can drive from Seattle to Boston on I-90, but if something forces us off portions of the road, or we learn en route that we must stop in Memphis, we might like to have a road map to save time, effort, and money and to arrive at the intended destination close to the original time and budget projections.

Succeeding in business requires a plan. A business plan answers three simple questions. So does a negotiation plan.

Business Plan Basics

1. Where are we now?

2. Where are we going?

3. How are we going to get there?

If all we want to do is beat the supplier down to a lower price, who needs a written plan? Just get out the hammer and let the bludgeoning begin! Balancing the elements of cost, creating a strategy, and selecting appropriate tactics suggest that enough is involved to merit the effort of a written plan.

The most logical place to begin the written plan is with the elements of cost: **Q**uality, **S**ervice, **D**elivery, and **P**rice (**QSDP**). Every pursuit in supply chain management rests upon the principle of Total Cost of Ownership (TCO); supplier certification and evaluation systems, terms and conditions, strategic alliances, and the negotiation plan all build upon the TCO foundation.

The question of just what is negotiable is a common threshold issue. The answer is all the elements of cost, QSDP. Return to the cost elements of last chapter wherein we broke down each of QSDP into sub-elements and weighted them as to importance for railroad ties. We repeat our findings here for convenience.

Concrete Railroad Ties

Quality
- Rejection percentage
- Useful life
- Scrap rate
- Remedy policy

Delivery
- Transportation
- Storage

Price
- Payment terms
- Price-change terms

Service
- Technical competence
- Electronic capability

We have previously designated Quality as the most important cost element. We will give greater weight to these elements in our negotiation. Delivery is the second most important element to us and has potential as a multiple-use bargaining chip. We know, even if we are not willing to admit it to the supplier, that we are willing to pay more for high quality because costly shutdowns in operations can be avoided by longer life cycles of the ties. Price and especially Service are relatively unimportant to our TCO model. These do, however, hold great perceived value as concession giveaways, especially Price. Sellers instinctively expect Price to be a sticking point for buyers. In this TCO model, Price is not of great cost to us. This very fact sets up a concession that we will soon learn how to make effectively.

Organize TCO issues in terms of importance.

A good rule to follow is to concentrate on the importance of issues, not the sequence of how they will be addressed. Our model above does that rather neatly. I learned this lesson half a lifetime ago, in one of the thankfully few legal imbroglios in which I have been entangled.

A customer had apparently decided that it was likelier that he could reduce what he owed by hiring a lawyer rather than convincing me to accept 25 cents on the dollar. Two distinct projects were involved, but they shared the same set of facts and revolved around the same issues. My lawyer studied and prepared for one case and persuaded me to do the same. On the first day of arbitration, the opposing lawyer pulled one of those questionable tricks and switched the 'apparently' agreed-upon order of projects. My unprepared lawyer was unwilling to lose face by not proceeding, so we did. The result was predictably poor. Clearly, the other lawyer was a better negotiator, even in the adversarial mode. The moral of the story has stuck with me: Always focus on the issues, not the sequence.

Another reason to heed this advice is found in other forms of human competition. As a youngster, I was not big or fast in athletics, nor particularly gifted. My greatest asset came in the form of determination. In high school football, the coach explained these facts of life to me. His words have been applicable in countless ways since. "Menard, you cannot overpower larger opponents, but you can use their assets against them. If the defender wants to go left, use his inertia to drive him left. It will be easier to push him than to overcome him. The ball carrier will see the hole you made on the right and take it. You will be there to meet him!"

Whether the opponent is following human urgings or deliberately trying to shake you off your game plan by focusing on issues rather than sequence, you will remain standing amidst the earthquake. Who cares about sequence anyway? Some folks want to start with big issues, and most with small, at least as those issues look in their lenses. Following their sequence may even make them more comfortable with the process, and often this comfort will translate to greater success.

Prioritize the Costs

The next step is to prioritize these costs so that we can map out our concession strategy. Concessions should never be made without careful preparation and analysis ahead of time. It is the recognizable hallmark of an irresponsible amateur to concede impulsively. For instance, in the example of railroad ties, we need to decide whether having the supplier stock ties for our exclusive use is worth our granting a price increase, or whether we could be more flexible with our remedies for nonconforming material if the supplier absorbed all scrap costs.

We will see that a critical factor in successful negotiation is to make concessions of high perceived value to the other side while these concessions have limited actual value to us. Before we get to that, we will graphically recap the basics of the negotiation plan.

Figure 3-1

The Negotiation Plan

Write issues down.

↓

Ignore the sequence.

↓

Organize in terms of QSDP (Costs).

↓

Prioritize Costs.
Most Important
Concessions
Least Important

A fundamental reason for a written negotiation plan is to map our concessions. If you think that making concessions is a sign of weakness, you might be right, but only under unusual or amateur circumstances. Poor concession behavior is the culprit. For instance, if we mistakenly concede as a sign of good faith, or to get the ball rolling, that concession almost certainly will be disastrous. If we are willing to give up early and big on a key point, then it surely must be a red herring of little actual value. Worse yet, we confuse the other side, who may earnestly be seeking a mutually acceptable solution to conflict. Our own ineptitude may be unintentionally but irreparably poisoning the negotiation well.

It is however, perfectly acceptable to concede first on small points, particularly if the concession has high perceived value to the other side. Perceived value in the negotiation sense, as opposed to the pricing sense, relates to the esteem placed on an individual cost by the other side versus our assessment of the value of that concession.

In order to explain and relate these concepts of concession and perceived value, it is helpful to introduce the widely known concept of high initial demands, called for convenience by its initials, HID. This practice of asking for more than we want is *de rigueur*, or necessary, in the negotiation world. Why you might ask, can we not just dispense with this dance and just get down to the issue? The answer is that there are, or certainly should be, many issues to negotiate, namely QSDP. We also do not yet know what the other side wants. This is much more of a problem when the sides do not know or have little reason to trust each other, as is often the case.

In a long-term, stable marriage between loving partners in which a high level of trust has been earned, HID (high initial demands) are usually not required and mostly ignored. The negotiating partners know their mutual interests and depend on the absolute honesty and integrity of their mates. In such cases, the negotiators can truly get right down to the core issues in record time and at minimum expense. How often is that the case in business?

Given the distance and healthy skepticism of business negotiations, we adopt a more conservative and cautious posture. Besides, sellers expect that the buyer has a moral imperative to 'beat them down,' at least on price. Therefore they must build in a margin to satisfy this red-meat hunger.

I have posed this scenario to thousands of buyers at seminars. Assume the position of the under-educated and under-trained buyer, which may not be a long reach from reality. We'll call you, the buyer, Tarzan. The sales rep, Jane, offers you a proposal largely centered on the Price of $100/unit. Of course, we have not done our homework and have no idea of our supplier's costs. Nevertheless, we bite for the bait and declare vociferously, "What do you think? I just floated in with the boat people? I won't pay more than $90 for that stuff."

Jane in sales cowers in Tarzan's presence and says that she must call her manager to get approval. This might possibly cost her job but you, Tarzan the customer, are worth the risk. Dutifully, she retreats to solitude (her Volvo) and calls Cheetah, her manager, on the cell phone. We have captured the conversation revealed here.

Jane in sales (barely containing her excitement)

> *"Cheetah, I am with that account you assigned to me with the chest-pounding buyer. He says that he won't accept a penny more than $90. You told me that I could go to $85. Help me out here, what should I do?"* (Tittering, laughing, guffawing and snorting fill the conversation void.)

Cheetah in management

> (Regaining composure) *"Jane, remember how we rehearsed this in training. You go back with your tail between your legs and say that I ripped you a new one. But, if he goes along and can double the order for delivery this month, just this one time, you can go along with it and still keep your job."* (Tee-he, ha-ha, etc.)

Jane in sales (Returning to Tarzan after a suitably long interlude)

> Jane takes her seat, head cast down in the presence of the superior customer. She explains, nay implores that Tarzan go along with Cheetah's message.

You get the idea. Fakery and lack of preparation leads to a fool's paradise where no one wins and resentment flourishes. So how does a high initial demand (HID) prevent that?

Perhaps the greatest luxury is the built-in allowance that HID makes for movement by both sides in pursuit of their goals. With Jane in sales above, her $100 HID permitted room to accommodate the unskilled buyer's predictable obsession with the price. Notice how she did it, though: She had to go through a whole routine in order to convey the importance of a concession that she had built in as a giveaway in the first place. Put that thought to one side because we need to cover other points first.

When you present an HID, you transmit a subliminal message that trains the other side how to treat you and thus establish their expectations. Take the example of how sellers have been training buyers forever that the higher the price, the better the quality. Remember the Price/Cost myth from Chapter 2? The seller has been training the buyer to accept the myth through HID. The buyer subconsciously expects greater value, somehow.

We have all experienced a more subtle example of HID at the grocery store. In the canned vegetable aisle, you come across the sweet peas. The national brand prices out at 89¢. Right beside it is an identical size can of store brand peas at a price of 69¢. What is your immediate impression? The national brand is better, higher-quality, tastier, sweeter, something, anything, but definitely better. It must be. The advertising says so in that catchy little song that you can hum in your head.

What do you really think about this, though? Does the store grow its own peas, or do they have the big national-brand private label for growing them? To verify your suspicions, drive around to the back of the store and see if you find any pea patches filled with pea pickers and pea packers. In all my attempts, I have never seen any. (For those who insist that the peas are different, substitute soap or paper napkins or shampoo or milk, etc., in the above example.)

The message the buyer gets is unmistakable. This is the powerful affect of HID. The chief benefit of HID is to prepare the marketplace for the fluid exchange of concessions. Not only does HID provide the room for movement, but it frequently provides the openings for exchanges or perceived value. This begs the question of what is a concession and how does it relate to perceived value and HID.

A concession or compromise is merely the exchange of one thing for something else.

In *Figure 3-2*, the first bullet point refers to high perceived value to them versus low actual value to us. This benefit is one of the vagaries and beauties of negotiation. High perceived value and low actual value is a direct consequence of Rule 2, each party does not want the same thing. The usual vehicle for accomplishing concession is through HID. An example will make this clear.

Figure 3-2

Concession

An exchange of one thing for something else.

- **Perceived value to them vs. actual value to us.**

- **Keep open mind when offering and accepting.**

- **Don't compromise ethics or principles.**

- **Start with smaller issues, smaller compromises.**

- **Never be the first to concede on a major issue.**

As part of our negotiation planning, say that we have identified Delivery as the most important element of cost. Price is second most important, followed by Quality and Service. We will use the principle of HID to deftly negotiate a better deal on Delivery, as well as to reduce other costs. Further, we will capitalize on the three critical levels in the concession strategy.

3   HID

2   Nice to have

1   Must have

We always begin planning at the bottom level with 'Must have,' because that is the absolute minimum acceptable position. Any result below that level means that we must seek alternatives to a negotiated solution. The 'Nice to have' position is a comfortable level above 'Must have.' It is a good idea to condition oneself to aim for the 'Nice to have' level, especially with new or untested suppliers.

The HID level can be whatever you think is appropriate. Unrealistic HID, while common, should be used judiciously. Outrageous HID can easily create the impression that you are unreasonable or abusive and encourage the other party to generate unrealistic HID's of their own. This is not a conducive atmosphere for negotiation. Therefore, use unrealistic HID sparingly.

For this procurement, we know that we absolutely need to have the purchased item no later than four weeks after the order. This is our 'Must have' position. Opening at the bottom would be foolish, in that the seller would regard any subsequent attempt to improve the lead time as a bad faith move. On the contrary, moving down from the HID is considered honorable and a sign of good faith. Remember now, we are working with a mixed bag of art and science in the realm of business negotiation.

A reasonable 'Nice to have' position for this procurement is three weeks, which would give us one week of float time. Choosing to be realistic, we opt for two weeks as our HID. We summarize the buyer's choices in the left-hand column of *Figure 3-3*.

Figure 3-3

Lead Time Concession

	Buy		Sell	
	2 Weeks	H.I.D.	5 Weeks	
	3 Weeks	NICE	4 Weeks	
	4 Weeks	MUST	3 Weeks	

"If I do that for you, what would you be willing to do for me?"

The seller's choices are opposite in direction. Its views are summarized in the right-hand column of *Figure 3-3*. Their negotiation planning shows that they absolutely need 3 weeks after the order to deliver. Their HID is therefore easy to establish at three weeks. A more comfortable time would be four weeks and thus the 'Nice to have' position is set. Choosing to be a little more aggressive, the supplier elects a HID of five weeks. The horse trading between customer and supplier might be as follows.

Customer (represented by *Ima Byer, Sr.*)

> *"Ivan, we like the quality of your products, but we need to talk about your delivery lead time."*

Supplier (represented by *Ivan Tasale*)

> *"Thanks, Ima. As you know, that quality costs us a bit, so I'd like to talk to you about a price increase that goes into effect next month."*

Customer (Ignoring reference to price increase)

> *"Well, if you can't get the stuff to us on our time frame, it doesn't matter if you provide it for free, so let's address delivery first. We need the stuff here in two weeks. Will you be able to meet that delivery?"* (Introduction of buyer HID)

Supplier (Choking back a chortle)

> *"C'mon, Ima, nobody on the planet can get that stuff to you in two weeks. We require five weeks."* (Introduction of seller HID)

Customer

> "No *thanks, five weeks will not work. We may have to keep looking if you cannot do better. What can you do for us?"* (Buyer allows seller the opportunity to concede on its HID to Nice to have.)

Supplier

> *"Ima, I am willing to go out on the limb for you on this one. Are you saying that we have a deal if I can get you your stuff in three weeks?"*

Customer

> *"Ivan, three weeks still makes life difficult for us, maybe impossible. I do not know if I can get my guys to go for this. But in exchange for you going out on the limb, let me try to return the favor. Help me get this deal through. If I can persuade them to go along with three weeks, what would you be willing to do for me?"*

This last sentence is a vital part of any negotiation strategy. Refer to *Figure 3-3* again and you'll find it at the bottom. The buyer's 'Nice to have' of three weeks is the same time period as the seller's 'Must have'. Would it make sense to agree to the offer in the spirit of equality, fraternity, and just to be a reasonable guy? We can live with the three-week delivery, and the supplier is trying hard to please.

A few pages ago, amid the discussion of HID, we cited the fuss that Jane in sales made over her concession to Tarzan. She had to go through a choreographed routine in order to convey the importance of her concession that she had built in as a giveaway in the first place. Let's revive that discussion because this is a very important part of concession strategy – one that encourages well placed concessions and makes them valuable investments in the process.

Jane in sales knew enough about negotiation that she should not roll over and give up the price reduction. We would do well to emulate her actions in our negotiation. Jane read Thomas Paine in high school. That famous patriot wrote in his essay, *The American Crisis, 1776*, that, "What we obtain too cheap, we esteem too lightly; it is dearness only that gives everything its value."

Heed these words of proven wisdom! If Jane had not objected, her concession would have had little perceived value. The fact that she built in the concession as a give away attests to her negotiation skill.

Perceived value has great significance in persuading the other side of the dearness of our sacrifice. In the present example, Ima Byer, Sr. knew that three weeks met his 'Nice to have' level of comfort. Byer might even have suspected that three weeks was Ivan's 'Must have' position. If Byer had jumped to accept the three-week offer,

Tasale might be confused about how important delivery was to Byer. Further, Byer now had a Broadway opening to lower the TCO. For instance, in return for getting his people to go along with the three weeks, Byer can suggest ways for Tasale to sweeten the deal. These suggestions can include: better payment terms, reduced price, longer warranties, favorable packaging, and any element of cost in the negotiation plan. Therefore, having a written negotiation plan and creating a coherent concession strategy based on costs are essential to success.

Thus we enhance or diminish the value of HID by our concession behavior. The "What would you be willing to do for me?" question may be thought of as a conditional concession. That is, the decision to grant approval is conditioned upon a further concession of the other side. Any advantage thereby gained, however, could be wiped out by other poor concession behavior. That brings us to another often mishandled form of concession behavior, that of how to control the size and direction of concessions. We will use price as an example.

As part of the negotiation planning, a buyer sets the top price she will pay or 'Must have' position at $10,000. The 'Nice to have' is $9,500 and the HID is $9,000. This buyer is knowledgeable about the purchasing landscape and properly estimates that the HID is reasonable. However, all of this advantage will be overturned by faulty concession behavior.

Figure 3-4 plays out the scenario. In the left-hand column, the buyer makes a minimal concession of $250, which the seller rejects. The buyer then over anticipates the seller's reaction and doubles the concession to $500, in the spirit of getting a done deal. The seller does not know the buyer's HID, but has just become intrigued with the buyer's behavior. Each time the buyer concedes the concession doubles. The logical next question is "What would the third concession be worth?" Is it reasonable to think that it might double again to $1,000? Of course, and temptation is too much to resist. Meanwhile, the buyer finds himself backed into his 'must have' position of $10,000, if the seller is merciful.

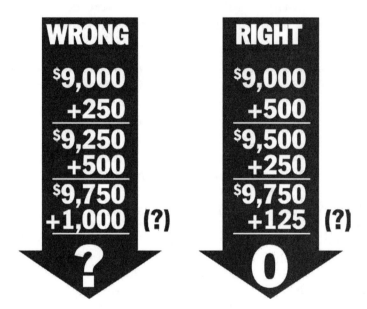

Figure 3-4

How Size and Direction Affect Concessions

The buyer has confused the seller with a poor grasp of basic mathematics and a worse grasp of psychology. Contrast that behavior with the alternative shown in the right-hand column. The buyer makes a big deal out of making the concession at all, and then offers a $500 concession if the seller can deliver earlier, or meet some other condition.

The seller might agree to the earlier delivery if its conditional concession can be met with a better price to sweeten the deal. Reluctantly, the buyer ups the ante again, this time with a raise in the price of another $250. Now the seller notices that each time the buyer concedes the amount halves. The logical next question is "What would the third concession be worth?" Is it reasonable to think that it might halve again to $125? The pattern is clear. The buyer is converging on the mathematical limit of $0. The message is silent, persuasive and inescapable. Meanwhile, the buyer finds himself at his 'Nice to have' position and in possession of other concessions that will lower the TCO.

Concession behavior is the very heart of negotiation. Poor behavior can derail the best negotiation planning. In the next chapter, we will consider other aspects of preparation as it relates to research. This emphasis on negotiation planning is deliberate. It stems directly from the fact that face-to-face contact consumes but a small fraction of our negotiation time. Most is spent in preparation and research.

Summary

TCO is the foundation of the negotiation plan. We use the relative values of QSDP to prioritize our costs and organize a negotiation plan. In the plan, pay attention to the issues, and not a presumed sequence of introduction.

The concession strategy is the heart of the negotiation plan. It is based on costs. We establish 'Must have,' 'Nice to have,' and HID positions. HID helps to create perceived value and provides the fuel for the concession engine. We make concessions in terms of size and direction, in a manner that does not ruin our planning. Conditional concessions are crucial to reinforcing perceived value.

Chapter 4

Preparing for Negotiation II

Preparation is so important that it consumes about 90% of our negotiation time without the other party being present. It is also an intensely "human nature"-driven pursuit, as opposed to a mechanical system.

Humans see what they believe. Two people with polar differences in outlook can witness the same incident and describe it in completely different terms. Their preconceived notions, or biases, have conditioned them to see the world through their own lenses. Political debates are ideal examples. Business is no different. Negotiation demands an open mind, and that is not easy. We will need to begin by acknowledging that some things we may have believed without question may be absolutely wrong.

Consider these two facts of business life. Banks will lend you money if you already have money, and insurance companies will cover you for risks if you don't have them. I remember coming to grips with these frustrations as a younger man, but I had to challenge my beliefs to realize this. Now it makes absolute sense. You present a prohibitive credit risk without money, which means you must find other forms of credit before you are 'bankable.' Similarly, the insurance company will not insure you against a loss you are likely to incur, at least not without an offsetting premium to hedge the risk. To paraphrase Will Rogers, It's not what Congress doesn't know that bothers me; but what they know for sure that's wrong!

All research on suppliers or customers must begin with the buyer asking: "Am I as smart as I look?" The answer is no, of course not, you would need to be twins. Most everyone over the age of 30 has long been resigned to the reality of knowing but an infinitesimal fraction of all there is to know. Even if we have a thirst for knowledge, how many of us in purchasing think of ourselves as researchers? Huge waves of information inundate us daily in terms of facts, opinions, and rumors. Do we sort through and critically evaluate that information in some structured fashion? Maybe not, because we have no handy framework to do so and not many of us have the luxury of too much time on our hands.

Conducting our own investigation is always best. When we actively seek out information, it is likely to be far more accurate, reliable, and useful for our purposes. We begin the research by writing down the ideal result of the negotiation plan. The ideal result is helpful as a planning device. Do it for your next five big negotiation challenges. As a teaching device in basic sales training, sellers learn to picture and describe in detail their ideal customer. They do this so they will recognize it when they see it. Military planners study the enemy to anticipate how they will react and estimate the capability and goals of their adversary. The same is true of our negotiation plan. The ideal result will be the standard against which we can measure our actual result.

Companies devoted to excellence epitomize this practice. One upscale national restaurant chain offers a prime example. They treat hundreds of restaurant evaluators to a series of free meals in exchange for detailed ratings of their restaurants. They supply a ten page inventory of food and service issues to appraise. Evaluators are told specifically to assume a top rating of 5 for every item and to mark the ratings down from there for specific shortcomings. The chain has identified their ideal levels of performance and wants to know from their customers what it must do in specific areas to attain that level. We would do well to emulate this drive for excellence.

Returning to the business nature of our work, recall the three questions of a business plan.

1. Where are we now?
2. Where are we going?
3. How are we going to get there?

We noted in the last chapter that all three must be answered to achieve a successful negotiation. Our research generates the answers to these questions.

The answer to the first question is found internally. Where have the wheels come off the wagon in our past dealings with suppliers? Have we driven so hard for price that we have cost ourselves money? Be prepared for reflections from the mirror that are not pretty. For instance, a long-term client has memorialized his favorite saying of what not to do by posting a banner in his office proclaiming, "We will get the lowest price no matter what it costs!" The moral of this tale is "know your costs," as we discussed in Chapter 2.

Research answers the second question, "Where are we going?" It is essential to know that or we can never get there. Remember the part in Lewis Carroll's *Alice in Wonderland* when Alice comes to the fork in the road and she asks the rabbit which road to take? "Well", the rabbit responded, "where do you want to go?" Alice then replied, "I don't know," to which the rabbit absolutely correctly pointed out, "Then, any road will take you there."

As business pros, we cannot afford to be as naïve or confused as Alice. We will see in Chapter 8 that this assertion is backed up by a legal responsibility as well. Our negotiation plan is the procurement equivalent of the company's business plan, and no less critical to success.

Suppliers constitute an immense portion of any business. In manufacturing, for instance, the dollar amount of purchased goods, services, and equipment can reach 85% of the sales dollar. Even at lesser percentages, the impact suppliers have on success cannot be understated. Wherever we are going in our business plan, we are getting there in tandem with these suppliers so it would be good if we knew our travel mates a bit better.

The answer to the third question, "How are we going to get there?" controls our negotiation strategy. How we approach the negotiation is a function of our estimation of the supplier's importance and value to us.

Supplier Certification Program

What form should the research take? One is Cost Analysis. Another is our knowledge of the supplier. It is a question in which name, address, and major product lines count as necessary but totally insufficient answers.

The best tool available to increase our knowledge of suppliers is a Supplier Certification program. A certification program sets minimum standards for doing business with us. Without it, we proclaim to the entire supplier world, "We have no standards whatsoever. If you have a pulse and a price, come on down and do business."

TCO lays the foundation for supplier research. We are most interested in traits or performance of the supplier having the greatest impact on the TCO. For example, if quality is our most important cost element and we find from our supplier plant visit it has no statistical process control in place or lacks a high-tech lab facility, this alone may be enough to disqualify a supplier. Our aim is to eliminate a problem before it ever appears. This is a proactive, cost-controlling measure and the antithesis of the fire-fighting mentality that pervades those businesses that have little understanding of TCO. Just reacting to a problem is not good enough. Bailing out your sinking boat will keep you afloat, but it does nothing to solve the problem. Yes, you must bail to survive, but it would be better to inspect the boat before leaving the dock. Supplier Certification avoids the leaks before the boat is swamped.

Figure 4-1

Supplier Certification

WANTED

TOP-NOTCH SUPPLIERS

- No "Pulse and Price" types need apply!

- These are our standards; if you can meet them...

- We commit to these Cost standards of QSDP and expect our suppliers to honor this commitment.

Figure 4-1 sets forth the rationale for certification. (Qualification and certification have the same meaning for our purposes.) In a moment we will create a simple certification program. But first, think of Supplier Certification as a negotiation technique.

Consider the effective psychological message your certification program makes. It proclaims a different and better sort of customer, one for whom quantitative cost impact is the criterion for doing business. It discourages slick pretenders whose major asset is talk. You have standards that must be met to get on the dance card. The immediate and irresistible challenge for a supplier who does not measure up is to improve at once or deal with our unsophisticated competitor. We also want to avoid doing business with the 'leak'-prone suppliers because these leaks are actually lost profits in the form of higher costs.

If your organization ever failed to qualify as a supplier, or lost a sale, or was disqualified from future business, you know all about the ensuing commotion. Everyone scurries about in the interest of improvement to soothe the sting of failure. Suppliers who fail to meet our criteria will experience the same motivation for improvement.

A Supplier Certification program's standards proceed directly from our recognition of costs. This is the importance of the program; the daunting challenge of how to institute it remains.

We begin by determining which suppliers have the most damage potential. Expressed another way, the suppliers with whom we do the greatest amount of dollar volume and therefore stand to create the greatest havoc, are prime candidates for certification. Rarely, a small dollar yet critical item may pose an inordinate threat, such as 'O' rings on the space shuttle, or shear pins on a continuous process pump. These suppliers must be certified as well but the overwhelming majority of cases will be the heavy hitters.

Let the 80/20 rule be your guide here. This rule is in reality a principle of economics attributed to the Italian Vilfredo Pareto (pronounced Pa-RAY-toe). Toward the end of the 19th century Pareto observed that 80% of the wealth in Milan was concentrated in 20% of the population. Borrowing from the Pareto Principle, we would not be surprised to discover that 80% of our purchase dollars are concentrated in 20% of our suppliers. It would be this 20% that would be the focus of our certification efforts.

Do not be distracted by the apparent sophistication of a certification system. I have had some very large Fortune 500 type clients who have answered, "Well, nothing formal" when I asked them to describe their systems. Some very small clients on the other hand have a bare bones set of standards that they apply to suppliers who fall within the pale of their core competency. So, the size of the company is relative. The amount of damage a body can endure depends largely on the size of the body.

The individual pieces of the certification program relate to many questions that we might not even have considered. We list some concerns here and briefly describe why these are important. This list is by no means exhaustive, but a basic checklist to establish a working knowledge of the supplier. The relationship to QSDP will appear in the Terms and Conditions that we will examine later in this chapter.

A Supplier Certification program can be viewed as a negotiation technique because it establishes an opening position. A thorough reference on the subject of supplier certification as well as supplier evaluation systems is *Purchasing Management – Guide to Selecting Suppliers* by William Obie Ford, published by Prentice Hall in 1993. Certification and evaluation systems are the province of purchasing management. They relate to negotiation to the extent that they provide useful information to the negotiator. Accurate information is the currency of successful negotiation transactions.

See Preliminary Supplier Certification Checklist on next page.

Preliminary Supplier Certification Checklist	
Category	**Reason or Caution**
Financial	Best way to spot a potential failure
Annual Reports	Summarizes history, future, trends, markets
Credit Information	Credit bureau info for private organizations comes primarily from the supplier
Audited Statements	Nothing else has the degree of integrity we need. Reject unaudited statements.
Management	Style reflected in company's operations
Organization Chart	The Who's Who of the organization
Style	**Entrepreneurial**: more agile and risk-tolerant Professional: more predictable
Longevity	Stability
Technical	Not just for high-tech
E-commerce ability	Speed, accuracy, productivity and cost-reduction systems
Market	The common-sense factor
Supplier size	Too small or too large may be a problem
Buyer size	Being too much of the supplier's book of business isn't good for either party
Price Analysis	*Essential*
Cost Analysis	*Essential*
Personnel	It's the people above all
Workforce	Union versus merit shop, contract expirations, harmony clauses
Training	Companies that invest in their personnel will probably value their customers, too
Outplacement	No help for their own people? Why would it not happen to their customers?
Turnover rates	High turnover is a sign of discontent.
Industry	No one wants to be the guinea pig.
Familiarity	Learning curves cost money.
Supplying our competitors	Could be either a good or bad thing.

Service	Is Customer Service really just Lip Service?
Order fulfillment	How are orders handled after placement? What can we expect or improve upon?
Service Centers	Location, hours, and capability
QA/QC, testing, etc	If the equipment is older than you are, discount all their quality claims.
Assigned reps & engineers	Will you get the same reliable person who actually knows what he is talking about?

What is the point of all this research? One objective is to make an intelligence estimate of the other side. What will be their HID and 'Must have' positions? What concessions can we expect them to make? Forewarned is forearmed, as the wise adage goes.

Another objective is to identify their hot points. What are they looking for as an ideal result? Since we know from Rule 2 that buyer and seller don't want the same thing, it would be helpful to our efforts to use the information we uncover to find the other side's motivations. We can then structure our concessions to meet these needs. A third objective is to separate their real issues from the straw issues that may be introduced.

The intelligence provided by our research allows us to make an estimate of the do-ability of the negotiation. Some negotiations are just not do-able. Buyer and seller will sometime be unable to reconcile their positions and agree. That is okay. If the cost is too high, we pursue other alternatives. Part of our negotiation planning is to identify an alternate route. Each party should develop a fallback strategy in case its negotiation efforts fail. *Figure 4-2* is a handy way of envisioning the results of your research in terms of do-ability.

Figure 4-2

The Do-ability Assessment!

Buyer	HID	$2.00	$4.00	Must Have	Seller
Nice To Have	$5.00	$7.00	Nice To Have
Must Have	$8.00	$10.00	HID

For illustration, we will take the case of price, although any of the QSDP elements could be substituted. In this diagram, the Buyer is shown on the left and the Seller on the right. The HID, 'Nice to have,' and 'Must have' are shown in inverse order to each other as the Buyer's HID will be low and the Seller's high. We have set the Buyer's HID at $2.00 and the Seller's at $10.00. Look next at the 'Must have' positions. It is essential to set out a 'Must have' position as this is the point at which no deal is preferable to a negotiated deal (because the TCO of the negotiated deal is too high, beyond what we can expect from alternatives).

If the Buyer estimates that the Seller will accept no less than $4.00 and the Buyer has established that he will pay no more than $8.00, a do-able negotiation range is identified. Both Buyer and Seller have 'Nice to have' positions in relative proximity within the do-able range, so this deal has a high probability of do-ability.

If the research suggests that the Seller will accept no less than $9.00, this presents a problem that must be addressed. This may be a deal breaker, unless the other cost elements can be reduced to bring the TCO into line. When Price is the most important cost element, however, as is often the case with commodity goods, it may be unlikely that other cost reductions will offset the price premium, which would make this deal not do-able.

Summary

Research and knowledge are essential components of the negotiation process. Preparation in the negotiation process consumes about 90% of the effort. A Supplier Certification program is, in reality, a negotiation technique that reinforces the TCO approach. Additional benefits are the reduction of problems before they arise and an estimate of the do-ability of a deal.

"Knowledge is power."

Francis Bacon

Chapter 5

Negotiation Strategies

Nothing arouses quite so much difference of opinion in Negotiation seminars and training sessions as the definition of Win-Win. Among the tens of thousands of participants, almost everyone professes it, only a basketful can define it, and still fewer actually practice it.

Coming in a close second in the consternation and confusion contest is the meaning of the 'Best Value.' The most popular response is "getting the most for the least." If "the least" means cost, not price, then this definition is not bad. We know from Chapter 2 that the 'Best Value' is the lowest Total Cost of Ownership. We have also seen that TCO forms the framework of our negotiation plan in Chapter 4. Our next task is to arrange our knowledge of the other side, the relationship, and interests, the issue, into a cohesive negotiation strategy.

Win-Win is the most popularly espoused strategy in negotiation, but not the only one available. Most of us would like to believe that Win-Win just happens, probably as a by-product of our hard work and dedication. Exactly why or how this mystery happens is not our main concern, because it is everyone's individual responsibility to take care of him or herself first. Presuming that the other guy also has this self preservation goal in mind, well, Win-Win must happen.

This is exactly the outcome produced by Adversarial Negotiation. The traditional us-versus-them philosophy dominates in business negotiations. But it is true that in the capitalist system we are all responsible for our own economic prosperity, so how do we reconcile these seemingly contradictory views?

The threshold challenge to confront is that one strategy does not fit all cases. Our societal preconditioning toward winning and losing, confusion of price with cost, and ignorance of TCO principles all lead to misguided negotiation behavior. Heck, Win-Win is not even appropriate or wise in some cases, so we need more than altruistic motivations to rule our decision as to how we will proceed.

Recall that Rule 2 declares that both parties don't want the same thing. This fact widens the field of possibilities to many fruitful outcomes. The TCO principle allows both sides to attain what they seek without harming the other side. In fact, they may help the other side reach its goal. It is exactly because we have Quality, Service and Delivery elements of cost to consider besides Price that makes Win-Win possible. Alternatively, if the two parties argue only over Price, then there must be a winner and a loser because only price is at stake.

Before we look at any strategies, let's be certain we understand the reliance of Advantageous Negotiation upon the TCO. By including Quality, Service, Delivery, and Price (QSDP), we have quadrupled the negotiation territory. In the past, the purchasing profession might have earned ill repute for fixation on price. It would be irresponsible to ignore price because it is one of the elements of cost. It may even prove to be the most important element as we prioritize the costs of the any one purchase.

This larger territory makes it easier for both sides to get what they want out the process. For instance, would you be willing to pay a price premium for immediate delivery? The iron and steel industry has recognized this impact on its customers' TCO model for more than a century. The price for immediate delivery from a warehouse almost always far exceeds the multi-month lead time for orders shipped out of a mill. This amounts to granting the supplier a price increase in return for a lower TCO.

In other cases, higher quality in the form of extended warranty provisions, replacement policy, upgraded models, longer useful life, etc., may offset the cost of longer delivery lead time. A supplier may tempt a customer with low prices for certain goods that are not moving well. Indeed, the buyer may bargain for further price reduction, because it lowers the supplier's inventory costs, making the deal good for both sides. The impact of TCO is a powerful influence in negotiation and must be in the forefront of our minds as we conduct business.

The selection of a strategy drives the negotiation. It will determine our tactics, concession behavior, and preparation. Tactics are purposely saved for last in this book because they proceed from strategy and consume a smaller portion of our negotiation efforts than does strategy and preparation. Strategy trumps tactics in military and negotiation planning.

We have four basic strategies from which to choose; Win-Win, Win-Lose, Lose-Win, and Lose-Lose. Our selection will derive from our assessment of the Relationship and the Issues.

Relationships

Relationship is expressed in TCO terms like dollars-and-numbers, not personal terms like empathy and friendship. A mythical but nonetheless renowned 20th-century business magnate, Don Corleone (The Godfather) sometimes opined that "It is just business, nothing personal!" Indeed, Signore Corleone used a mixture of negotiation strategies, dictated by his relationship to the other side.

In our business dealings, relationship means a willingness to continue doing business in the same fashion because it yields desirable results. If we are each satisfied with our dealings, and we want to continue to do similar deals in the future, then the relationship has high importance.

Issues

Issues are strategic interests such as competitiveness, market initiatives, and corporate leadership mandates. Any forces determining the direction of the organization are issues. For instance, suppose that we are a high-cost producer of a mature product in a mature industry. Assume further that sales are down, losses are up and executive management announces a cost-cutting program to return to viability. Cost reduction is the issue and commands high importance.

It is the balance between the importance of the issue and the relationship that determines our choice of negotiation strategy.

Figure 5-1

Negotiation Strategy Matrix

The matrix in *Figure 5-1* shows a convenient way to picture the four strategies and the conditions that control selection. The importance of the Issue is shown horizontally across the top, increasing from right to left; greater importance at the left and less importance at the right. The importance of the Relationship is shown vertically on the side, increasing from bottom to top; greater importance on the top and lesser on the bottom. The graphic is further augmented by identifying who wins and who loses; another detail that sometimes gets lost in imprecision.

Folks can reasonably ask. "Doesn't it depend on your point of view? That is, the other side does not know what I want, so how can they know if I win?" The answer is that we can help the other side win because we don't want the same thing (Rule 2). Win-Win can occur exactly because of the inclusion of QSDP into the process.

When the issue and the relationship are both important, the appropriate choice of strategy is Win-Win. Similarly, when the issue is more important and the relationship less, then Win-Lose is the choice and so forth, according to the chart. We will next take a closer look at each of the four strategies.

Strategy: Win-Lose (lower left quadrant)

Win-Lose is the strategy most frequently practiced. Many negotiators who profess a Win-Win strategy actually believe that all that matters is that they win. Perhaps the other side will win, too, but that happenstance is strictly incidental. Sports competition conditions us to this belief, because at most events there must be a winner and a loser. You can almost hear the growl of the primitive instinct, "And I'm not going to be the loser." The Win-Lose negotiator is a Tyrannosaurs Rex, whether in lamb's clothing, silk suits, or denim jeans. T-Rex cares little for anyone but itself and wastes copious opportunities for Win-Win as it tries to clean the negotiation table of all scraps of victory. Some of the telltale words of T-Rex are, "Better luck next time," or "We'll make it up on another one," or "You did a fine job." Sure, T-Rex wants you around the next time it smells blood.

Yet, this strategy is perfectly appropriate for certain conditions. According to the chart, the proper time to use this strategy is when the issue matters more than the relationship. Then you want to win, and you don't care if they lose. A good example is many labor negotiations. Assume that manufacturing company XYZ is losing market share to overseas competitors because Third World labor costs are a fraction of US-based operations. XYZ has even weighed the option of locating a plant overseas to stay competitive. The issue of competitiveness is more important to the company than the relationship. Indeed, if the company does not become competitive, the relationship will have no value because

XYZ will be out of business and no one will be working. Win-Lose is the best strategy to pick for this type of circumstance.

Another example is the US airline industry. After the September 11, 2001 attacks in New York, the major airlines suffered disastrous losses that ultimately led to multiple bankruptcies. As each domino fell, executive management approached labor unions with "take it or leave it" demands for concessions. If the unions did not capitulate, the airlines threatened bankruptcy, where neither party would be in charge of their fate and union contacts might well be repudiated by court fiat. Clearly, the issue of survival was more important to the airlines than the fate of their unions.

Since most negotiators will in fact reside in the Win-Lose quadrant, expect that you will face many sellers whose only strategy is Win-Lose. Sellers may justifiably believe that their customers are not truly converted to the TCO faith. If you find that most of your negotiation strategies fall into the Win-Lose category, you may want to reexamine the wisdom of repeatedly fighting the same battles. We will elaborate more about this in the Win-Win strategy discussion.

Strategy: Lose-Win (upper right quadrant)

Lose-Win strategy is the one most foreign to purchasing pros. A major reason for this is the illusion that buyers are in the driver's seat in negotiation and therefore wield the greatest power. Horse hockey! If buyers have all this power, why are we negotiating with the sellers? We negotiate because they have something that we want.

A most uncomfortable posture for most buyers is to assume the role of the sales person. Even though it is wise to walk a mile in the other guy's shoes, buyers do not relish the prospect of becoming a salesman, even for fantasy purposes. While I can easily convince a group of sales pros of the wisdom of donning the buyer's role, it causes near revolt when I whisper the suggestion that buyers try to imagine being sales people. So let's do it.

Suppose you are a top sales pro with several key accounts that you serve and protect with the dedication and devotion of a soldier. Since your key customers are so valuable, you have worked with your management to continuously reduce costs, whether or not the customer always appreciates your toil. Nevertheless, the relationship with one key account has cooled, and you fear the worst. Orders are down, communication is strained, and competitors are stealing orders. You request a meeting to clear the air and finally get a confirmed date. You cool your heels for about an hour before being directed down the hall toward the buyer's office. The buyer is on the phone as you approach. Your chair is across from her desk. It is low to the ground, uncomfortable, and if you sit there, you will be blinded by the sun streaming through the open blinds. Given all of these conditions, what should you do?

Buyers rebel against this scenario because we do not like to admit that we are guilty of such behavior and probably feel that the seller deserves such treatment anyway. Therefore, responses from buyers to this question are predictably belligerent. These include moving the chair out of the sun, sitting on the opposite side of the desk with the buyer, adjourning the meeting site to a more neutral location, remaining standing, and closing the blinds. All of these actions reveal a take-charge attitude, invoking a power show down. Such aggression aligns more with a Win-Lose strategy and underscores an ignorance of the Relationship and Issue matrix.

Sales pros, on the other hand, being more experienced with T-Rex behavior, innately understand that assertive actions are counterproductive in this situation. The buyer has set the stage to be in control and wants the seller to know who is boss. The seller has a clear picture of the strategy matrix and recognizes that the long-term relationship matters far more than the buyer's control issue. If the seller accepts the buyer's ploys, rather than inflaming the conflict with counter measures, the buyer may then be able to voice her concerns so that the seller can set about solving the problem and salvaging the business relationship. By "succumbing" to the buyer's trick, sitting in the low chair in the blinding sun, the seller has made the wise choice to lose the battle in order to win the war with this valued customer.

Strategy: Lose-Lose (lower right quadrant)

This strategy seems rather odd at first. It raises the question of whether and why any party would ever willingly intend to have both sides lose. Does the matrix graphic fail as a model in this case? The answer is that this strategy, while rare, does indeed make sense under appropriate conditions. These conditions are when the issue and the relationship both have little importance. An example will clarify the scenario.

Suppose that you are assigned the duty of buying photography services for the company outing in June. You receive this assignment on Memorial Day from the Human Resources folks who have been setting up the event since Christmas. In your sourcing search, you discover that every bona fide photographer has been booked for months to do weddings, family reunions, and graduations. The only photography service you can get is two college physics students, whose long-term career plans involve photographing gamma wave radiation! This is a clear-cut demand for the Lose-Lose style. Who cares about the Relationship? It has no future. And as for the Issue, do you really want high-resolution photography of employees who have overindulged all day, maybe kissing the wrong spouse?

To be sure, the conditions under which Lose-Lose is appropriate will be few, but it is the advisable choice in those rare instances when issue and relationship have little value.

Strategy: Win-Win (top left quadrant)

Now we arrive at the quadrant that garners the most attention, or at least loudest lip service. We already know about how Rule 2 stipulates that we do not want the same thing. A buyer may want a steady supply (Delivery) of superior goods or services (Quality) from a reliable supplier (Service). If so, then it makes economic sense to pay a premium (Price) to that supplier because we will benefit by the overall lower TCO. In such a situation, both parties would get what they want while helping, not denying, the other side what they want. Later in this chapter, we will examine the proposition of how continuous practice of Win-Win with good suppliers leads, in fact, to lower prices.

Win-Win is possible when the issue and the relationship both rate high importance. Think of this strategy as the basis for a marriage, a long-term, committed relationship in which issues tend to have mutual importance. Each party has a vested interest in the issues and in maintaining the mutually beneficial relationship.

A business analogy to marriage is the trend toward reducing the number of suppliers. The motivating force behind the reduction in the supplier base is the corresponding reduction in costs. This translates to an increase in profits for both buyer and seller. As the number of suppliers is reduced, the amount of business of the remaining suppliers increases, providing a ready basis for win on the supplier's part.

These negotiations tend to occur between parties that enjoy long-established relationships built on trust and mutual benefit. The business value ranks high in importance because each party enjoys profitability and wants to continue on this path. As to issue, each side will have different motivations. For example, the buyer seeks superior goods from a reliable supplier on predictable schedules. The seller may seek a higher price and that price may be cost justified. That is, it may cost the supplier more to maintain inventory for the buyer, or produce high quality, or maintain a service crew, all of which add to the cost and are represented in a higher price. The overall cost impact is however, a lower TCO than the buyer can obtain from less qualified, higher cost suppliers.

As a general rule, one-shot deals do not apply in the Win-Win quadrant. No relationship has been established, no trust built up, and no history of mutually beneficial profitability established. You would not marry someone you dated once, at least not without a high degree of risk. The same is true in business. One-shot deals belong in any of the other three quadrants.

Another unique feature of the Win-Win quadrant is that it carries a reward that cannot exist with any of the other strategies. This reward is the reduction in price as well as cost. Heretofore, we have been talking about paying a price premium in return for better quality, service and delivery. But with the constant practice of Win-Win comes the mutual reward to both parties of lower price. How can lower price benefit the seller? Let's look at this observation closely because the consequence is not obvious.

Assume that we have qualified our suppliers for doing business, as set forth in Chapter 4. A bonus feature of certification is that we have limited the suppliers with whom we do business to those who generate acceptable TCO levels. From this qualified list, we can further pare down the list to candidates for the strategic alliance of partnering. Partnering is not for everyone, indeed not for most. This buzzword has almost as many definitions as practitioners. In sales, partnering is sometimes viewed as a customer protection device to corral customers and keep poachers away, while adding some vaguely quantified added value. That thinking won't work for objective, dollars-and-numbers purchasing pros. The only acceptable reason for pursuing partnering is a reduction in the TCO. Partner suppliers are those who contribute to the customer's core competency, supply essential products or services, and who characteristically account for a great share of the buyer's purchase dollar. So how does all this contribute to a lower price?

Comparison Chart of Sales and Profits

Non-Partnering		Partnering	
Sales level $1,000,000	Costs	Sales Level $2,000,000	Costs
Material	$450,000	Material	$800,000
Labor	$450,000	Labor	$800,000
Total Cost	$900,000	Total Cost	$1,600,000
Profit Percentage	$100,000 10%	Profit Percentage	$400,000 20%
Negotiated Partnering Solution	Reduce prices by 5% thereby reducing sales level by 5% to $1,900,000. This reduces profit by $100,000 to $300,000 or 15%.		

The chart shows the effect on costs and profits for a potential doubling of sales for a partner supplier. Assume that this supplier's performance has been good enough to earn the reward of a 200% increase of its sales. The increase will come about mostly as the result of eliminating higher cost suppliers as we trim down the number of suppliers from the list. As part of the on going negotiation process (Rule 3), we examine the supplier's cost structure to ascertain the impact when sales are doubled.

Typically, a greater book of business brings savings to the cost side. We sometimes obliquely refer to these savings as 'the economies of scale.' These economies of scale have dollars-and-numbers explanations, so let's identify exactly what we mean.

In almost all cases, the costs do not increase proportionally to sales. That is to say, a 100% increase in sales may require only an 88% increase in costs, as illustrated in the example in the chart. From a production point of view, the supplier is able to purchase its materials at more favorable prices and to schedule its work longer in advance, shifting to lower cost facilities, etc. The supplier can drastically reduce his burden expense because he has a committed book of sales applicable toward retiring expenses. That is, the supplier's general and administrative burdens are now divided by a larger sales number, thereby decreasing the percentage. He also saves on sales, marketing, travel and advertising expenses that he would otherwise incur in chasing replacement business.

These reduced costs generate higher profits, twice the percentage in the case at hand. Given this cost picture, and a Win-Win strategy, it is appropriate and smart for the partners to discuss how this additional profit can be shared. One way is for the supplier to reduce his prices because he has lower costs. If he reduces what he charges by 5% to the $1,900,000, that $100,000 reduction will reduce the profit to $300,000. At this level, the supplier still nets 15%, which is better by half over his profit percentage at the lower sales level.

Thus, the Win-Win strategy offers a way for partners to reduce costs and prices. Each obtains greater rewards than would be possible without the willing input of the other. The customer doubles what he buys from the proven reliable and valuable supplier in exchange for reduced prices. The cost reduction provides the economic incentive to reduce the price without the supplier being financially harmed.

Summary

The term Win-Win means that issue and relationship both rank high in importance. The other appropriate negotiation strategies are Win-Lose, Lose-Win, and Lose-Lose. These are perfectly applicable, depending upon the circumstances. *Figure 5-1* gives us a handy reference to select the best strategy.

When the Relationship and the Issue are both important, the only appropriate style of negotiation is Win-Win. In all cases involving major customers and suppliers, and in partnering arrangements, Win-Win should be our only choice of strategy. Partnering leads to cost reductions which result in price reductions.

> *"There is hardly anything in the world that some man can't make a little worse and sell a little cheaper, and the people who consider price only are this man's lawful prey."*
>
> John Ruskin

Chapter 6

Communication Skills

Among all human endeavors, communication skills are the most essential to our species' success. This complex medium of information exchange is fraught with perils such as misunderstanding and confusion. It can be argued that our advanced human communication systems have made all other forms of societal progress possible. Without the ability to speak, listen, read, write, and intuit, we might still be loin-clothed foragers and hunters. Unlike almost all other features of evolution where rules are uniform and independent of the user (fertilization in agriculture, physics in engineering, chemistry in medicine, etc.), communication rules differ from person to person. Government is a good example. The chaotic process that distinguishes the democratic governments of the world exists because of the range of communication messages they embrace. Dictatorships sometimes are more coherent because only one viewpoint is tolerated. Listening in on the House of Commons in London on television will convince anyone that communication skills are a highly individualized enterprise.

What is the meaning of the expression, "Do you know what I mean?" It could be an earnest inquiry as to the mechanics of comprehension of the spoken words; i.e., was it sufficiently audible, clearly enunciated, and expressed in a language and words familiar to the listener. This might be the case in limited circumstances, such as of two people speaking in other than native languages to each other. More than likely, in the American corporate culture however, the expression; "Do you know what I mean" is not a question at all, but a statement of conclusion.

The implied message is "I am certain that you agree with me. Surely, if you heard and understood me, you must agree. The language was so impeccably elegant and the logic so precise that only someone of limited intellect could not agree." In this and innumerable other instances, the meaning of the words, the intent of the speaker and the comprehension of the listener convey three distinctly different messages.

Communication is a complicated subject. Negotiation is merely a subset of communication, the stage upon which negotiation is played out. The two-way street of communication runs to polar extremes; it facilitates rapid and efficient success while at the same time erects roadblocks and digs potholes that cause breakdowns of the negotiation process. In this chapter, we will study communication with the goal of conducting successful negotiations. Due to the complexity, we will address many techniques and show how to apply them.

We classify the elements of communication into two broad categories, literal and figurative. Literal elements are the customary communication forms of speaking, listening, reading, and writing. The figurative elements are the less tangible but equally powerful media of an open mind and of body language. We are more aware of our competence in the literal elements and tend to ignore the mysterious qualities of the figurative as a form of voodoo. We need to focus our attention on both to negotiate effectively.

Literal Elements of Communication

Most of us have studied the literal elements in school. We took language studies like English, Spanish, written composition, oral presentations, and literature. We have acquired the practical basics of all of these, but that fundamental level, while necessary is not sufficient for our negotiation purposes. Now we need to critically examine the mechanics and human influences of communication on the negotiation process, beginning with speaking.

Speaking

Most people shun speaking, questioning the innate ability to communicate effectively or skill at elocution and logic. They may doubt a depth of vocabulary, fret over an accent, or remember disasters. The list of worries tops out at public speaking, so daunting a practice that it routinely beats cancer on the list of maladies Americans fear most. Organizations and clubs like Toastmasters International exist to help people overcome the affliction of fear and inability to speak well. Clearly, this challenge needs attention.

One of my clients employed a fellow who fancied himself quite the wordsmith. During one of our team negotiation sessions, he was so adamant about his contention that the property being offered was such a piece of junk that he characterized it priceless! Everyone knew he meant to say worthless and an epidemic of covering of the mouth swept through the room as we tried to conceal our mirth. In another example, I heard a reference in a televised political speech to the Latin phrase meaning therefore, consequentially or hence. The four letter word he meant to say was "ergo," but unfortunately he got tripped up in his Latin and pompously prefaced his conclusion with the words "ipso fatso." If he intended humor, he certainly succeeded. The actual Latin "ipso facto" would have been a comical misapplication, but close enough for understanding. The malapropism "ipso fatso" sent people into hysterics and ruined the fellow's message.

In still another example, I remember a fellow explaining to me how his uncle suffered from psoriasis of the liver. I am sure that he meant to say cirrhosis of the liver. These instances are embarrassing and would lead anyone to shun occasions to speak in public.

More mundane instances could be the garbled toast at a wedding, the company meeting that drones through mounds of information, or simply the conversation that you cannot understand without multiple clarifications.

A recitation of some techniques will be helpful in improving speaking skills. Questioning is a speaking skill and a negotiation technique. How we question others in negotiations makes an enormous difference in how the information is received, processed, and answered. Prime examples are the open-ended and close-ended questions.

Technique: *Open-ended and close-ended questions.*

The open-ended question is designed to elicit information or encourage dialogue. It calls for an informative and involved response. The close-ended question can be and should be answered with a yes or a no. It is designed to enhance precision or weed out non-essential or even misleading information. Suppose you are in the market for equipment to increase productivity, reduce costs, improve safety and save on utilities. An open-ended question to pose could be, "Can you tell me how this equipment will help increase productivity, reduce costs, improve safety, and save on utilities?" If the sales person says "No," throw him out. A "Yes" answer must immediately be followed by detailed explanations in response to your inquiry. The open-ended question will occur more often in the exploratory stages of negotiation.

As the territory narrows, the close-ended question comes to the fore. Precision is gained by asking tightly defined yes or no questions. "Does the unit qualify as US-made under the 'Buy American" clause?" is a close-ended question requiring a clear, unequivocal response.

The close-ended question also clarifies details and pins down people you think might not be acting entirely candid with you. For instance, assume that you ask, "Can we have this unit in our Chicago facility 90 days from today?" If the answer is, "Well, we can ship it 10 weeks after receipt of the order and down payment," you have work to do. Remind the respondent that the answer calls for a yes or a no. In either case, you have made progress. If no, and under no conditions, you will need to look at extending your deadline or at other alternatives. If yes, you can then get more finite with the specifics to make that delivery date happen.

Technique: *'I' and 'You' statements.*

Everyone has heard the country expression that "It ain't what you said; it's just how you said it." Contained ironically in the adage is a demonstration of the 'you' statement. Consider these two statements of equivalent message. First, take the 'I' statement. "As

I understand what I think you said, thus-and-so would be preferable to you. Do I have that right?" The statement accounts for the possibility that we misunderstood, did not fully appreciate, or otherwise failed to recognize all the significant data under transfer. This tacit admission by us conveys the notion that it is important that we understand the sender's communication, its issues and motivations so that we can deal with it. This is what the social scientist call empathy, and that is a good quality in negotiators. We expressed no agreement nor disagreement, or even much positive or negative emotion. Rather, we proffered a down the middle statement of fact and asked for affirmation of meaning.

Contrast that with this imperious alternative 'you' statement. "You mean to tell me that you want thus and so." Imagine this being said with the accompanying finger pointing as well. Clearly, the 'you' statement lets fly an accusation and invites retaliation. The 'you' statement needlessly inflames the conflict that negotiation is intended to resolve (Rule 1). We will see in Chapter 9 how some negotiators use this type of language tactic to create a diversion in the negotiation by invoking a defensive reaction, then denying that anyone made accusations. Our motives may be pure, our intent to ensure that we understood, but our words of communication derailed our good intentions. In general, it is a good practice to substitute the 'I' for the 'you' statement.

Technique: *Reflective response.*

The reflective response simply takes the words you heard, translates them into equivalent terms and requests affirmation. This technique fully recognizes that two or more people can hear the same words and come to different conclusion as to what was said. If you don't think it is possible for two people to hear the same words, know the individual meanings of the words, yet come to vastly different conclusions, then consult someone who is married for a second opinion. Not only do individual words have different meanings but usage varies, some people speak poorly and our own prejudices get in the way of clear communications. If someone says O.J., your response might include the words orange juice. If they meant O.J. Simpson, your reflective response would clear that up before you got any further down field. The use of the reflective response in tandem with the 'I' statement are some of the most plentiful and powerful negotiation techniques you will deploy.

We can sometimes be confused by the tone of voice or individual delivery styles. For this reason, it is advisable to question the speaker about intent rather than impart our own meaning. For instance, suppose someone says, "Well that's just great." The meaning could be literal or it could be the ironic opposite. The tone may be used by the speaker to indicate frustration, disgust, anger, pride, or other conclusions. Such statements call for open-ended questions on the part of the listener. Fortunately, the spoken words of our verbal language leave clues of the speaker's meaning independent of the tone.

Verbal clues come unexpectedly. Let's take them on in the same staccato style in which we are likely to encounter them. Keep your ears attuned to these words when they pop up in negotiations because they usually signal important meanings or information that is worth pursuing.

Technique*: 'but'.*

The 'but' word is a verbal eraser of everything that comes before it. How many times have you heard interlopers jump in with the prefaced excuse, "I am no expert on that, but..." What is the next sentence out of that person's mouth likely to proclaim to the world? He is ready to demonstrate what an expert he really is, irrespective of qualifications. As my father loved to say, "Why clutter up a good argument with facts?"

The use of 'but' may also send the other side scurrying for weapons to counter attack this new revelation. We can clean up our act by substituting 'and' instead of 'but'. "I am no expert in negotiation and here I am negotiating with you, so please help me out." Instead of connoting challenge or flattery with the 'but' word, we have ratcheted down the conflict level.

Technique*: "I'm sorry'.*

Be on alert for these words of apology. Why would anyone apologize in advance for what they are about to say? The effect of the phrase 'I'm sorry' is to erase the words that come after it. It trivializes the speaker's words to the extent that they may be ignored. If the sales person says, "I'm sorry, our policy won't permit returns," she has expressed half hearted agreement with the policy, connoted an air of weakness and invited further resistance. Reserve the words 'I'm sorry' for mistakes.

Technique: *Changes in speech patterns.*

Train your ears to perk up when someone speeds up, slows down, repeats, answers a question other than what was asked, or otherwise changes their cadence. These departures from the usual betray a loss of poise that bears exploration.

When a speaker speeds up, they may be unconsciously trying to get past the trouble spot. If they whistle past the graveyard, maybe you won't notice they are afraid.

Sunday morning news programs serve up a bonanza of suspicious speech patterns. All politicians worth the office know the value of answering whatever they want to say, no matter the question. It is a way to get the message out, stay consistent, and avoid off script traps. Unless you are negotiating for public office, this circuitous route may not be the best. When faced with the politician negotiator, ask the same question in different words to eliminate any honest misunderstanding. Suppose, for instance, that you ask your spouse, "What time is dinner?" In response, you hear, "Well, I put the roast in at 4:30." This is an honest misunderstanding caused by answering a question other than what was asked.

Ask close-ended questions to improve precision. Perhaps insert the 'and' instead of 'but' word to clarify, and include the reflective response, too, such as in this sentence. "And you expect that roast will be ready at about what time?" You have narrowed the funnel quite a bit without creating any undue friction. As a last resort, explain your frustration and ask for help. If you receive none, your suspicions are confirmed. Often times, depending on the individual's personality, a seller may not want to answer a question head-on for fear of offending someone, betraying a confidence, or general insecurity. This is an interpersonal matter that is addressed in Chapter 7.

Technique: *Announcer statements.*

Announcer statements encompass a variety of prefatory remarks intended to condition the other side for desired effect. Off-the-cuff terminology comparable to "By the way" or "As you know" sometimes inadvertently introduce important or decoy information.

The preface, "To be honest with you" merits particular attention. On its face, the phrase is ridiculous. Is the speaker confessing dishonesty up to this point? That is probably not the intention, but it may be the message received. It should alert the listener that significant information probably follows.

The use of repetition sounds another announcer alarm. Politicians repeat for emphasis, or maybe because they expect people not to listen so they won't notice the repetition. Constant repetition, however, may be an indication of importance of the repeated point. It might simply be a flaw in negotiation skills. In any event, it bears clarification.

Technique*: Avoid pronouns.*

I know of nothing more prone to confusion than the overuse of pronouns. They (referring to pronouns) are just too non specific. The pronouns 'he', 'she', 'we' and 'they' are tough enough, but 'it' comes in for special scrutiny. A description that goes on for more than three sentences needs to reconfirm the identity of nouns being supplanted by pronouns. Any more than one male in a story and the use of 'he' becomes troublesome. Given that 'it' covers almost all creation, the pronoun problem (it, meaning the pronoun problem) cannot be overstated.

At home, I live with a wife, two daughters and a cat, all female. With my back to the crowd, I will hear, "Did you see how she did it to her?" ...Huh? Unless the house is on fire, I tune out all the static noise rather than try to unravel the pronoun references.

Technique*: Distinguish observation from conclusion.*

This fault of logic must be one of the most common problems for familiar parties. If someone offers an observation, do not impute your own conclusion. It may not coincide with his or hers. If the seller says, "We can not sell at that price," it is merely an observation. To furnish our own conclusion would be erroneous. We cannot summarily conclude that the price is too low. It could mean their costs are too high, or that the seller has some other controlling factor that is not divulged. Clarify the conclusion by asking straightaway what conclusion to draw. If the person is challenged by direct questions, employ the reflective response and rephrase the observation. Then, with the 'I' statement, ask about the conclusion. The talk might go like this. "So, if I understand the statement, that price is not available. Is that right so far?" If you hear a no, investigate with open-ended questions. If the answer is yes, the test for a conclusion might be, "So that I am clear, is the conclusion that the price is too low to cover the costs?" If the answer is yes, then switch to the Cost Analysis tool. This process of negotiation is an interconnected set of wide-ranging skills!

Listening

Thus far, we have been discussing the literal element of speaking. Listening is not the reciprocal operation of speaking. It is an entirely different and in many ways unrelated skill. It may be the secret weapon of many negotiators, because most of us do not know how to listen. In informal polls of groups, I have found that less than 1% of people have ever studied listening, formally or casually. We humans tend to believe that listening skills come naturally. After all, we have been doing it all our lives. Well, hearing is a more accurate verb, because listening is in some doubt.

The major difficulty with listening skills is that ears can hear faster than mouths can speak. Resort to numbers for clarity. The average American English speaker talks at the rate of about 125 words per minute (wpm). We can hear and understand about three to four times more than that. Can you recall the FedEx ad of the 1980's with the fellow talking rapidly about "getting the package to Pittsburgh?" Questions remain about the audio tape's speed of about 500 words per minute, but the speed speaker had a moment of fame, even appearing on The Tonight Show with Johnny Carson, and FedEx had begun a string of memorable ads. I remember the challenge of trying to listen to what he said. Little did I think of it as a negotiation skill test! I focused intently on what he was saying, shut the lights off, shooed the kids and dog out of the room, and I could understand him, for the most part. The point is that I devoted my complete attention to what he was saying. Given this observation about communication skills, answer this question: When a speaker is talking at the average 125 wpm rate of speed, and we are not exhibiting undivided attention, what are we doing with the other three quarters of our time?

Here are the four responses I receive most often and are validated by studies I have read. In order, they are:

1. Daydreaming

2. Forming hasty decisions

3. Making mental arguments

4. Filling in with busy work

The reason for daydreaming being most predominant stems from the practical mechanics of attention span studies. The repeating sine wave has troughs and crests. We are on high absorption at the crests and in deep fantasy at the troughs. It is just a fact of human nature and a factor impeding our efforts to negotiate effectively.

Forming hasty decisions springs from our internal prejudices. We all have them. We tune out someone because we know what they are going to say. "She always says that," is one telltale sign.

Mental argument simulates the challenge response. Something that speaker said strikes a chord, be it harmonic or dissonant, and we want to respond. If we agree, we are planning our response, just waiting for them to take a breath so we can jump into their spot and say, "Oh yeah, well I can top that." If we disagree, we may cut them off in mid-sentence, so angry are we that they dare spread such propaganda. "Oh, yeah, that is not so, and here is why," is a fairly typical retort that one might interject.

Busy work is what we do between times when it occurs to us that we should be using our time more efficiently. Examples of questions that arise are, "Did I distribute copies of that report?" or "Whose turn is it to cook dinner tonight?" and "Did anyone pick up the dog at the groomer last Saturday?" Some of us justify this under the euphemism of multi-tasking. Multi-tasking is counter productive to the cause of good listening, so save it for the company picnic.

All of these shortcomings in listening skills affect our ability to negotiate. Short of enrolling into a formal seminar, which is often worth the price of admission, a practical way to improve listening skills is to watch political talk shows. No matter what your stance, training yourself to listen to the polemics of the characters you'll find on these shows is an education in listening and in how to separate wheat from chaff, both of which are essential for negotiators.

Now that we have become more familiar with speaking and listening, we can appreciate the complexity of the human communication model. The model in *Figure 6-1* is adapted from the military to represent the dinner table. It illustrates the disarming complexity of communication and the constant need for clarity.

Figure 6-1

Communication Model

Issuance (Sender)
"Please pass the salt and pepper (to me)."

Receipt and Confirmation (Receiver)
"(I understand that) You want me to pass the salt and pepper (to you)."

Ratification (Sender)
"Yes, pass the salt and pepper (to me)."

Notification (Receiver)
"(I'm) Passing the salt and pepper (to you)."

This simplified model breaks down a complicated process. The complexity of human communication plants landmines to destroy the message both in the transmission and receipt. The military cannot afford failure. A mistake calling in artillery support can be disastrous. In the above example, the parenthetical clarifications are a source of failure. In less formal settings, such as the dinner table, we tend to omit the personal pronouns and get sloppy with the words. This leads to great confusion. We assume that the Sender wants the salt and pepper passed to him, but that is not necessarily so.

In our negotiations, we want to be careful not to assume what the other side wants. We often stop the process after the Issuance stage. We presume that everyone in earshot must know what was meant. This mistake is related to the listening fault of forming hasty decisions. "He always wants the salt and pepper" may be our reaction, but not warranted in this particular case.

Technique*: Establish expectations.*

One of the payoffs of improving listening skills is that it trains the negotiator in establishing the expectations of the other side's demands. Instead of automatically assuming that we know the other side's position, it is far better for both sides if the other side states and stakes out its position. I was fortunate to learn much about dispute resolution in the 1980's while serving as an arbitrator in court appointed and contractually agreed cases. In the 1990's, I served as a mediator in dispute resolution. Arbitrators cannot participate in settlement talks, because they may have to impose settlement, while mediators are active advocates in settlement talks. One of my first objectives was to establish criteria. To my amazement, the complaining party (claimant) had a far different claim than had been put forth in the proceeding. The complaint alleged all kinds of damages and sought remedies of actual, compensatory, punitive and "other compensation as determined by the proceedings". In our initial talks, the claimant divulged to me that he really did not want to pursue anything but payment of the balance of the contract. If it was paid within 45 days, he would be satisfied. The respondent, who also claimed huge amounts of counter damages, similarly had no appetite for protracted wrangling and jumped at the chance to drive a stake through the heart of this dispute. Claimant and respondent settled that week and continued to do business together. Fortunately, I did not assume that what each party wanted was as stated in their claims. As is often the case, positions are far less important than motivations.

In order to tie the speaking and listening skills together, we probe one more example of human communication fallibility. Early in this chapter, we noted that the meaning of the words, the intent of the speaker and the comprehension of the listener have three distinctly different messages. We call this the three levels of meaning in anyone's speech. These are:

1. What the speaker says

2. What the speaker thinks he is saying

3. What the listener thinks that the speaker is saying

These three levels of meaning must be recognized in any communication, let alone negotiation. In fact, this communication mechanism is the reason that we need to deploy tools like the reflective response, 'I' and 'you' statements. It is not possible to always have these three levels overlap. Moreover, it is more likely that the more familiar negotiators are with each other, the greater the odds for confusion because we assume that we know what the other side means. Here is an example taken from the domestic scene.

One hobby that my youngest daughter and I share is cooking. One night, my 10-year-old and I were preparing pasta primavera. The vegetables were done, the sauce finished, and the pasta al dente. The cooktop is on an island in the kitchen. With my back to her, I could not see that my daughter had set up the colander in the sink. As I removed the steaming pot from the fire, seeing my daughter in my peripheral vision with her back to me at the sink, I growled, "Clear the sink!" Let's apply that one sentence to the three levels of meaning rule.

1. "Clear the sink!" That is what the speaker said.

2. What the speaker thought he was saying were words to the effect that his daughter should move away from the sink so he would not risk scalding her.

3. The listener thought, quite to her consternation and confusion, that her father wanted her to remove the colander from the sink.

Similar scenarios play out multiple times per day in our personal and professional relationships and are in need of our deliberate attention. A good habit to adopt is to give level number three the most weight in communicating. Think of the listener as the customer. It is the customer's opinion that matters most in business relationships so let this be your guide.

The other two literal elements of communication are reading and writing. For most of us, these have far less effect on negotiation than do the other two elements, and therefore, far less treatment in this book. Reading is usually done in connection with the research aspects of preparation. Due to the process of negotiation (Rule 3), the information gathering is continuous. If you are not in the reading mode and have little spare time, the news here is good. Academic volumes on the economics of supply chain are not as beneficial as are business magazines, trade journals and newspapers. For a professional buyer, subscriptions to Purchasing Magazine, The Wall Street Journal, and a half dozen trade and technical journals should be part of your regular reading. You can glean substantial information in articles of less than about 1,000 words and can consume more of those than you can doughnuts in the time it takes to sip your morning coffee.

One absolutely essential caveat about reading is that you must read everything that you sign. Preprinted documents, a technique called Sacred Writings in Chapter 9, is one of the most powerful persuasions in business. It suggests that these printed words are beyond reproach and must be accepted as written, with not so much as a stray making. Bull feathers! Among the authorities of negotiation, Herb Cohen pointed out this fact in the title of his 1980 classic, You Can Negotiate Anything. I once refused to sign a release form for the auto dealer to work on my car. This action was in fact a negotiation stratagem because the document had business consequences. It was two pages of six-point type that I couldn't even read, much less understand. The service writer could not explain what the document meant. He referred me to the service manager who didn't even bother with explanations. She just tore up the form and told me my car would be ready at 5:00 p.m. That experience taught me this negotiation technique.

Technique*: Never accept a 'no' from someone who cannot say 'yes.'*

This is not as obvious a statement as it might appear. The feint of putting lightweight personnel who can only say 'no' in the apparent position of authority is a very effective tactic used by all kinds of customer service organizations. Part of the justification for this predominant roadblock is that some customers cheat and will use any excuse to chisel on payment. Sometimes, however, the motivation can be rather ignoble. We will take this purely theoretical example to make the point.

Suppose that you complain to your cell phone supplier about questionable time usage charges. Your daily reading research uncovers newspaper and magazine articles about a class action suit against the phone supplier. In testimony, the phone company has admitted 'some overcharges' due to delays in billing for minutes from rented signal towers that have "forced" them to "push minutes into inappropriate and undue billing periods". While not the customers' fault, they are charged for exceeding their contracted monthly limit, despite the phone company's complicity, unless the customers are alert enough to spot the mistake and savvy enough to challenge the bureaucracy.

Suppose further that the phone company hires a collection agency to harass customers. The collection agent only has the authority to remove outrageous late charges and not to mitigate the undue balance, or even admit that the balance is phony. In this case, dealing with the collectors would be fruitless. They don't have the authority to settle the dispute for the correct amount. You would be taking "no" from someone who doesn't have the authority to say "yes."

As far as writing, very little negotiation is done in writing except to the extent of pre-printed documents foisted upon the unwitting who may not be aware of the tactic. A good practice to observe is to request any forms, terms and conditions, contracts, etc., to be forwarded in advance so that you may review them and perhaps send them on to your lawyer for vetting. As a tactic, some buyers like to reserve these forms until the last minute and produce them to the seller as a fait accompli during face-to-face sessions. Whether that is a good or a bad thing depends upon whether one is the buyer or the seller. While it may be acceptable for us to do it, we do not want it done to us, so request them in advance.

Figurative Elements of Communication

As we turn the corner to the figurative elements, we move from tangible nuts and bolts to the mysterious and imaginative. The two major concepts here are body language and an open mind. Some mastery of both is essential to negotiate effectively.

An Open Mind

When I ask folks to stand up if they refuse to have an open mind, every one remains seated. Of course, because an equivalent question would be, "Who here is a close-minded bigot?" We like to think of ourselves as open-minded. We are not sure what it means, but it sounds good. Diplomats joke that tact is the ability to tell someone he is open-minded when they really think the fellow has holes in his head. For negotiators, open-mindedness is the realization that many outcomes are possible, depending upon your point of view.

As an exercise in open-mindedness, answer this close-ended question with a 'yes' or a 'no.' Specify a rationale for your answer. "Is it possible for a physical object to be moving backward and forward at the same point in space and time?"

For assistance in our answer, we invoke the expertise of no less an authority on such things than Albert Einstein, the 20th-century physics genius. The folklore behind Einstein's inspiration for his theory of Special Relativity is as follows. Einstein was standing on the quay of the train station waiting for his laboratory assistant traveling on the approaching train. Nearing the station, it became clear that the express train, which his assistant had mistakenly boarded, would not stop at the local station. At the exact point in space and time that the express train traveled at 100 km/h past Einstein's point of view, the assistant's suitcase lashed to the top of the train became dislodged. Einstein witnessed the suitcase hurtling forward, in the direction of motion and momentum. At that very same point in space and time, the lab assistant traveling on the train looked up and saw his suitcase hurtling backward, away from the direction of his motion, decelerating from its previously imparted velocity of 100 km/h. Clearly, both men were correct in their observations. The suitcase was moving forward and backward at the same point in space and time – it all depended upon the observer's point of view.

The question of moving backward or forward is the exact equivalent of whether we are a buyer or a seller in the negotiation. Keeping in mind the dominant importance of Rule 2, however, we enjoy a benefit not available to the physicists. We can move forward and achieve our agenda without moving the other guy backward. This fact makes negotiation one of the most rewarding pursuits in business.

The open mind brings a bonanza of techniques that are beyond the reach of our closed-minded brethren.

Technique: *Dumbness.*

Without any doubt, dumbness is every negotiator's best friend. It represents the most beneficial affect of enjoying an open mind. Dumbness does not mean abject, grunting ignorance, but the subjugation of one's prejudices, beliefs and ego. As an entertaining and loosening ice breaker in crowds, I often ask, "Is anyone here as smart as they look?" Suspecting a joke, an occasional brave soul will raise his or her hand, to which I remark that "You couldn't be -- you'd have to be twins!" We are not as smart as we look. As Clarence Darrow is said to have once noted, "I don't pretend to know what many ignorant men are sure of."

Technique: *Never agree or disagree with explanations.*

This caveat is especially true of statements of opening position. Openers are notoriously overstated (such as in the arbitration case noted above), sometimes intended to inflame, and sometimes as a counter wrought of over estimated assessments of the other side's position. It is far better to understand the motivation than to argue with the position, at least at first. When you are presented with a seemingly outrageous position, think to yourself, "What an interesting attempt." You may well be ready to laugh or walk out in a huff, but that would not exhibit much open-mindedness.

Suppose that you are presented with this initial position statement: "You know as well as I do that our product is making you a ton of money and costing us a fortune. We have to get double what you are paying now." Our concern should be for the motivation, not the position. Is this supplier losing money? Are we at fault, or did this supplier willingly low ball us for internal purposes? Was the supplier trying to trap us on the ship and then raise the fare when we left the dock?

First, we know from the dumbness technique that we don't even know for sure what we think we know, so how does this other guy know that he knows what we know as well as he does? Secondly, double the price sure sounds like a lot, but the supplier just mentioned price and cost problems, so let's make him prove his case before we do anything. This leads to the next technique.

Technique: *"Tell me about it."*

The 'never agree nor disagree' technique above has just landed you a Broadway opening for sweeping questions about the supplier's cost and price structure. Recall that we discussed Price and Cost Analysis in Chapter 2. We pull out these tools and bring them to the table immediately. Recall also in Chapter 3 that we discussed the dominance of the issues over their sequence. The course of any negotiation is virtually unpredictable and thus the stress we place on planning. In this instance, we seize the opportunity to inquire, with our sophisticated questioning techniques, about the Cost and Price Analysis angles. In fact, a flatly stated, matter-of-course response should be "Tell me about it." We should use this one as often as a plumber uses a wrench.

Technique: *"What-if"* questions.

This technique is a reflection of the open mind because it implies flexibility, creativity, and a willingness to entertain divergent views. It does not signal acceptance, and it encourages experimentation. You might even find nuggets that you can use or did not expect to pan out. For example, suppose that the supplier's high quality is adding unsupportable costs to you. You ask, "What if we were able to accept a lower quality; would you be able to supply that and what would be the impact on the price?" The supplier might not be able to do anything, but that sales person has learned a valuable lesson about your willingness to keep an open mind and will reciprocate at his first chance. Or, that supplier may jump on the chance to contact his sales management and engineering people for a list of alternatives. The seller may have sufficient inventory of equally high quality material left over from a production overrun. It is slightly off spec for our purposes, but the supplier offers to underwrite the cost of testing to see if we can use it. If we can, the supplier offers a 50% discount to move the inventory. Should this exercise in open-mindedness work out, both sides will have actively participated in a Win-Win strategy.

Keeping an open mind does not come naturally. Our instinctive reaction is to take self-preservation measures. We prepare to defend ourselves and advance our position as our prejudices, beliefs, and narrow minded conclusions dictate. HID is one example of this self-protective instinct. We assume that we have to start at some point higher than where we expect to end. This is not a bad thing, but while prepared for the battle, we cannot afford to foreclose on other choices. So, how do we balance our open-mindedness? One handy tool is to frequently listen to extremists. How do we recognize an extremist? Why, the extremist disagrees with our opinion, of course.

Identify someone with whom you have vast and animated political differences. It does not matter what opinion, as long as it is opposite yours. We do not listen because of the normal daydreaming, hasty decisions, and mental argument problems. In most cases, all that would result from listening to an extremist is that we will be all the more convinced of the wisdom and righteousness of our viewpoint.

However, it is also likely that we refuse to listen out of fear. We worry that the extremist may say something with which we agree, maybe heartily so. Were that to happen, we would be forced to reexamine our value systems and that is a frightful prospect. I once heard an anti-American extremist (that is how bad he was!) making a point about foreign policy. Upon consideration, I had to admit that his perspective might be a possible explanation. At least, I could understand how he might think that, although I was certain that his point had no factual or sensible basis. But if it did, I might be forced to reassess my convictions about a whole range of issues and question how I came to these values in the first place. Upon some investigation, which I would not have done otherwise, I finally did dismiss his thoughts as propaganda. We will miss out on opportunities if we refuse admittance with a 'Mind Closed' sign on the door.

Body Language

No treatment of figurative communication skills can omit the mention of body language. We purposely draw attention to the study of this discipline because it is a separate and thoroughly deserving body of knowledge. Body language is so fascinating because its scientific findings are subject to artistic interpretation. This leads to individual differences in particular and imprecision in general.

The study of body language also requires live demonstration or resort to extensive visual illustrations. Both options are impractical in a book of written words. In much the same way that the mastery of medical science includes knowledge of related fields like pharmacology, mastery of negotiation requires knowledge of body language. Everyone I ever met who has studied it enjoyed the effort. Make the acquisition of a book, attendance at a seminar, or online study a priority in your personal pursuit of negotiation skills.

Summary

Communication skills are complex and the greatest source of breakdowns in negotiations. For simplicity, we categorize them into literal and figurative elements. The literal are speaking, listening, reading and writing, and the figurative are body language and an open mind. All are sufficiently complicated as to deserve further independent study. Negotiation is a subset of communication skills. Our success depends largely upon our effective communication skills.

Practical techniques contained herein should be liberally deployed throughout our negotiation efforts.

Chapter 7

Interpersonal Factors

"Negotiation would be great if it were not for the people!" Do you know anyone who thinks similarly -- someone in the mirror, perhaps? It is a natural and completely understandable statement of frustration. Since we people only negotiate with other people, this problem is not likely to go away. People with whom we negotiate have different personality types and behavior quirks that confuse, anger, distract, and amuse us. As practitioners, we can not be passive observers about interpersonal factors. We are interested in managing problems and producing results.

Let me offer from experience that people drawn to the purchasing profession do not generally come pre-programmed to deal well with interpersonal factors. Most of us toiled in related technical and scientific pursuits such as accounting, engineering, and production, where we did well due to our resourcefulness and creativity. Then, we had the good fortune to be assigned to purchasing. Put another way, our reward for that success was a sentence to purchasing. In our prior careers, we generally dealt with processes instead of people. A system or a machine reacts a lot more predictably that do people, even people whom we know. For those of us who fall into the left-brained category, think of this chapter as remedial reading for the interpersonally challenged.

Now that we have admitted our weakness, how do we go about

conquering the interpersonal factor beast? We turn to the Golden Rule of Negotiation for guidance. We all know the more familiar biblical golden rule that sets forth unassailably sound morality about individual actions. "Do unto others as you would have done unto you" is timeless advice.

Personal interaction in negotiation settings, however, is more intellectual than physical. As such, we must modify the Golden Rule to suit. Our modification on the theme sets a stage more conducive to negotiation by recognizing that intellectual messages are a lot more subtle than physical messages. The Golden Rule of Negotiation is "Do unto others as they would have done unto themselves."

Negotiation is far more practical than theoretic. For example, I pose this question for your consideration. As a practical matter, do we prefer the company of people who are similar to or different from us? "Tell me about it," you might say from reading the last chapter, to which I respond, "Bravo!"

We tend to prefer the company of those who are similar to us to that of those who are different from us. We are more comfortable with those who share our values, our beliefs, and our general view of life. In a fashion similar to our prejudice toward extremists, we doubt and fear the view of the world exhibited by those who have personality types different from ours. By using our open mind, we can turn that inherent disadvantage into a strategic advantage in negotiation. Call that Advantage Communicating in the other guy's language.

All sales training introduces the concept of buying motivations early in the process. Sellers are taught that no one buys unless he judges the purchase to be in his best interest and that the buyer's question is, "What's In It For Me (WIIFM)?" This portrait of buying behavior may not flatter buyers with nobility, but it represents a popular view among sales people of the buyer's personality.

In Chapter 4, we spoke of making an intelligence estimate of the other side. Sellers do this by estimating their answers to the buyers' WIIFM questions. This preparation helps in evaluating the do-ability of the deal, establishing HIDs, and concessions. We still must deal with the people and personality issues, overcome communication barriers, and observe the Golden Rule of

Negotiation. In this chapter we concern ourselves with a mastery of personality styles and how they relate to effective communication.

The social sciences have produced volumes of studies on the complexities of personality issues. We will draw upon a portion of these studies and narrow down the material to suit our limited purposes.

Many folks have had personal experience with personality profile tools and instruments such as Meyer-Briggs, Keirsey, and the DiSC, among many others. These sophisticated studies are best left in the hands of professionals for all but limited purposes. We will do just that as we distill these works to their essence for application to negotiation.

Fortunately, we do not need to be social science experts to be effective in our negotiations; in the same way that one need not be a nutritionist to know how to eat healthily. Our communication skills matter far more than our ability to identify and manage personalities. Expressed in relative terms, communication skills are more useful than personality skills in negotiation. Nevertheless, personalities are important to the extent that they dictate how people communicate so we need to know more about the subject.

A personality is a composite of multiple styles. We call upon a style depending upon the stimuli of the situation. For instance, aggression surfaces naturally when we play competitive contact sports, but not when we watch the graduation ceremony at the day care center. The personality of the CEO is probably much different than the research engineer. So too will be their communication styles. The Golden Rule of Negotiation tells us that we need to approach them, sell to them, and buy from them in the manner that they, not we, find appropriate.

Figure 7-1 is an iteration of thousands of similar graphics you have probably seen. It shows four basic personality types defined by the extremes at each end of the axes.

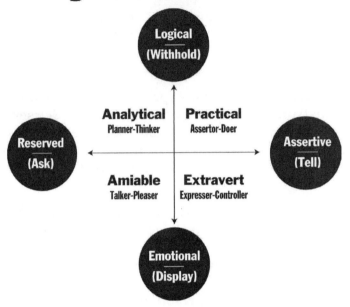

Figure 7-1

Negotiator Personalities

This adaptation of personality studies applies to negotiation for a specific reason. Rule 1 of Advantageous Negotiation tells us that "Negotiation requires and resolves conflict." Conflict involves stress. Stress invokes the fight-or-flight response. Our animal instincts gravitate toward strength when we face this primal response. Greatly simplified, we resort to our strength when facing stress. Our dominant personality type tends to be the major force we summon to confront important challenges. Therefore, if we can identify the dominant personality type of our negotiation counterpart, we are able to estimate how best to communicate with them.

Refer to *Figure 7-1*. Call the vertical axis the Reason/Emotion line. It is the rough equivalent of left brain at the top, and right brain at the bottom. Logicals have strong rational traits, favoring thoughts over feelings. They withhold emotion. Emotionals have strong humanistic traits and favor feelings over thought. They display emotions.

Call the horizontal axis the Assertiveness line. The Reserved folk prefer asking, even when making demands, while the Assertive ones prefer to tell, even when asking. The axes intersect to create four personality zones. These zones provided ample clues to their communication preferences.

In the upper left live the Analytics. This zone's markings are high reason and low assertiveness. They think carefully and methodically and favor charts, graphs, and reams of supporting documentation. They prefer to read and study in advance rather than to hear the information on the spot. They do not get very excited, are cautious about their vulnerability, act consistently, and generally hold their cards close to the vest. Plenty of engineers, accountants and other process-oriented personnel fall into this zone.

In the upper right dwell the Practicals, who are high on reason and assertiveness. These are the ones who are prone to snap decisions. Typically, they are in a hurry, even while relaxing. This commander does not let facts stand in the way of a decision because instinct is a good enough substitute. Their driving personalities dispose them toward goals and competition; they welcome challenges, take control, question authority, and want immediate results. Bosses, leaders, and high-level managers in positions of responsibility populate this zone.

In the lower right reside the Extraverts. This zone encompasses high emotionalism and high assertiveness. The Expresser types share some traits with the Practicals in that they too are impulsive, and competitive. They however enjoy limelight and excitement more than results and prefer creativity over reality in problem solving. They value feelings and relationships. Human Resource, customer service, and sales professions are comfortable in this zone.

In the lower left, the Amiables thrive on high emotionalism and low assertiveness. They like conformity to the groups and they follow rules readily, do not believe in follow through, and need reassurance. They ask many questions. Agreeable, supportive and polite, they have difficulty making decisions because they want to please people. They often change their conclusion because the last viewpoint was the most influential. Negotiation is not high on the list for folks in this zone to pursue.

Based upon wide experience, I offer an empiric observation about personality types. The majority of purchasing and sales pro personalities is in the Analytical, Practical and Extravert zones. Further, more purchasing types trend toward the two logical zones (Analytical and Practical) and more sales types trend toward the two assertive zones (Practical and Extravert). It makes eminent sense in the traditional roles that buyers would be the engineers, accountants, bosses and high level managers who favor processes while sales pros are assertive, people oriented relationship types.

We said that the zone of one's predominant personality type provides ample clues about the communication style. Since that is the most important reason for identifying the personality, we will examine how to approach each with *Figure 7-2*. *Figure 7-2* resembles the previous chart except that it is modified to reflect communication style with a simple geometric symbol.

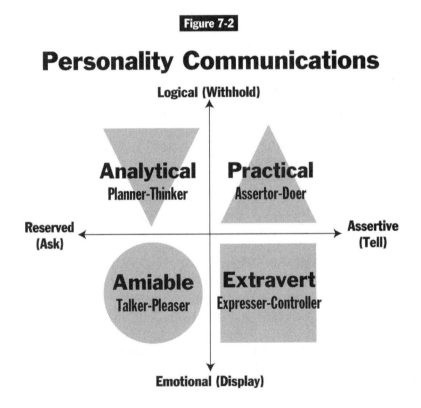

Figure 7-2

Personality Communications

Logical (Withhold)

Analytical
Planner-Thinker

Practical
Assertor-Doer

Reserved (Ask)

Assertive (Tell)

Amiable
Talker-Pleaser

Extravert
Expresser-Controller

Emotional (Display)

Suppose that we are negotiating with an Analytical. His communication style is represented by the inverted triangle shown in that zone. All information presented must flow logically and have plentiful supportive backup so that logical conclusions are made before advancing to a deeper level. We know he prefers order, would rather get things right than done, and has a keen eye for details.

How do we treat the Analytical as he would do unto himself? Certainly, flashy shows designed to induce emotional reaction such as visible body language signals will fare poorly. Contentions lacking substantive, written back-up will be seen as irresponsible and be dismissed. Above all, do not get straight to the point! Sales people should not pose closing questions until very late in the process, for instance. A clear, fact-laden and documented argument must be made before any such attempt. Doing otherwise invites failure.

The Practicals communication symbol is the news article pyramid shown in that zone. In a news story, the writer sketches the main points first, starting with the headline which states the conclusion. As the reader progresses, supportive facts appear in increasing detail. This style is designed to allow the reader to cut off at the point at which the reader judges that he has enough information.

How do we observe the Golden Rule of Negotiation in this instance? Above all, be brief. State the case clearly and succinctly up front. If you are selling (and we all sell to the boss), get the WIIFM across immediately. Be prepared for a decision to be made at any time. Don't worry about hurting feelings – you won't. Practicals do not tend to take things personally unless identified as such. Accordingly, do not expect small talk or social niceties; it is nothing personal, strictly business.

No matter how gifted we may be at recognizing personality styles, and applying effective communication skills appropriately, we must constantly hone our talents. My wife is an Analytical, and I am a Practical, so let me opine from a position of great experience.

Trained in medicine, she knows about charting and analyzing copious amounts of disjointed information. For instance, she routinely researches the minutiae of dosage schedules, medication interactions, and disease processes. No off-the-cuff diagnoses need be offered by casual outsiders. The epitome of the inverted pyramid communication style, she soaks up the specifics, assesses the value and applicability of the data, studies the documentation, and tests each hypothesis before narrowing down to a logical conclusion. That is a good thing for her profession. Her communication style is in absolute harmony.

When she speaks to me about almost anything, however, she follows the same communication pattern because that is where she is most comfortable. She explains in excruciating detail all of the factors that could possibly be relevant. She'll add in information about how some person acts, or what the process or system is at issue, and who the peripheral players are and the amount of their input. Sometimes, I fully expect to hear the names of the children, the birth order, and how that might be relevant under certain alternative scenarios. As a Registered Nurse, she does terrific work. As a negotiator, she is a work in progress.

As a Practical personality, I share many of the characteristics common to inhabitants of my zone. The pyramid model is a godsend to me. As a junior high school student, I learned with amazement and satisfaction that the proper study method included, indeed required, that one read the chapter summary first. This technique facilitated learning and aided the procedure of simplifying and summarizing that is so crucial to education. That was an absolute epiphany to me. I had been toiling all wrong up to that point. There I had been, slogging it out word by word, getting lost in the details when I really should have been summarizing and condensing. I even thought it was cheating to read the summary first!

When my wife launches into her protractions, it is not my impatience, or listening failures, or prejudice that is the major problem. The problem is that I cannot follow the story. All the players, the situations, the influences all suit her communication style, but not mine. It reminds me of playing Clue as a kid. I was never good at Clue, and for much the same reason. One must be squarely in the Analytical zone and have the wherewithal to keep all the data straight. I would guess it was Professor Plum in the kitchen with a lead pipe and get person, place and weapon clues wrong. Nothing much has changed about my personality, and nothing much will change with the people with whom we negotiate, either.

The Amiable is a foreign concept to Practicals. We cannot fathom how someone can function with low assertiveness and high emotionalism. It is opposite to everything that we know. I apply the techniques that I learned about asking non-threatening questions, expressing feelings in stories, and not rushing the Amiables. However, in short order, I find myself frustrated with their inability to take risks. How risky can it be to answer the question, especially if I assure you that it won't hurt my feelings? That is why the symbol for this personality zone is the circle. It simulates circular logic and circumlocution that accompanies this style of communication.

I once interviewed a fellow who obviously had taken extensive sales training. He either was a true Amiable or was trying out his techniques, but I could not get the guy to commit to the time of day. Reaching into the questioning techniques toolbox, I forced the conversation to close-ended questions. I asked if it came in blue, to which he replied, "Would you like it in blue?" I asked if we could have it in our west coast facility by 60 days from today. He replied, "Would you like it 60 days from today?" Finally, out of amusement as much as frustration, I asked him if he could make the sun rise in the west tomorrow. He thought about his answer but demurred. Perhaps he was too afraid to hurt my feelings if he told me I had the sun's path mixed up.

The Extravert zone is most troublesome for the Analyticals. They cannot figure out how one functions in the high-emotion, high-assertiveness style. Extraverts volunteer their opinions and ideas, even when these thoughts are not quite coherent, logical or realistic. The symbol applicable to this zone is the square. Extraverts stand as four-square advocates for their ideas. They are proud to express them. They can start anywhere in a story and finish anywhere because it is the relationship, the feeling, that matters. The feeling will be the vehicle that leads to the result somehow.

Sales pros often exhibit Extravert tendencies, including a tendency toward control. They must be assertive because sales is a tough business. Think of how many times they must hear the word "no" in a career. They need high emotional equipment to establish relationships with a variety of customer personalities.

When attending to some financial matters during the boom years of the late 1990's, I had the opportunity to speak to several high-powered reps of brokerage firms. Over dinner, one fellow made unrealistic projections and promises. Pulling out the open-ended questions, I dug for justification information on how such claims would be accomplished. The more we worked on the individual claims, the more reasonable shape the projections took. By the time we had finished, we parted company with a clear understanding of an investment plan that that was reduced to writing the next day. He approved with no changes the memorandum of understanding that became the basic document for our investment plan. The document bore little resemblance to his salesman's puffery and totaled only about one-third of the assets he envisioned and upon which he based his assertions. Nevertheless, the next time we spoke, he repeated his claims as if we had proceeded under his original plan. It does not matter where the Extravert starts, as long as they finish with the relationship.

Buyers are likely to meet many Extraverts in negotiation. One of the best tools buyers will ever use in managing them is the Supplier Certification concept we developed in Chapter 4. Certification and its logical consequent, Supplier Evaluation, deal with the numbers-and-dollars approach that business should always exemplify.

Summary

Interpersonal skills matter because they define a negotiator's communication style. Negotiation is a stressful event. Under stress, we resort to our strongest behavior type or dominant personality. We are all a conglomeration of personality types. For negotiation purposes, we can think of personality types as confined to four zones: Analytical, Practical, Extravert, and Amiable. Each has certain traits, depending upon how assertive or reserved, logical or emotional that individual personality behaves.

Chapter 8

Practical Legal Considerations

Why include a chapter on legal matters? The most common goal of a negotiation is to reach a contractual agreement for the exchange of goods and service for other value. The agreement for exchange is a contract and thus our interest. Our motivations are entirely practical. Bringing in legal talent for every deal would bog down the process, raise the cost, and needlessly strike an adversarial tone. Parties react anxiously when attorneys accompany or especially lead the negotiations. Parties themselves suffer from internal friction when the lawyers (often justifiably) feel that they are being tied down with details that competent purchasing pros should be able to handle. Lawyers have a valid argument that they are legal advisors to other capable professionals. Finally, deals for illegal subject matter, or between incompetent (a legal term) parties can be challenged on enforceability or good-faith bases.

I am not a lawyer, nor do I play one in seminars or in books. Nor is this chapter intended to substitute for sound legal advice. Rather, it is intended to complement the lawyers' contributions. One need not be an attorney to acquire a working knowledge of commercial law. You must, though, be equipped with the basics so that you can spot dangers and refer those trouble spots to competent counsel. That is the purpose of presenting this material, and it is limited to the practice of negotiation.

Experientially, in my years of consulting, training, and education work with purchasing pros, I have found the gaping ignorance of commercial law to be the most widespread deficiency. I came to the stunning realization that a better knowledge of the law was mandatory in this fashion. One manufacturing firm that I served was a hard-driving, career consuming organization that valued its people according to the amount of slavish dedication to duty they exhibited. The highly compensated crowd was expected to put in 60 to 70 hours per week. The executive crew comprised of the president, CEO, and a handful of other key personnel, would meet on Sunday mornings for strategy sessions. Alan, a real life S.O.B. (son of boss), ran these meetings. At one session, I presented the results of a computer-sorted run of customers against suppliers because I had discovered that we had substantial overlap. Moreover, in general, we purchased far more dollar volume from these suppliers than we sold to them.

Alan suggested that I corner these suppliers with this ultimatum: "If you want us to keep buying from you, you'd better double what you buy from us." Well, by golly, that seemed like a gem of a plan to me. As the head of purchasing, I could boost sales and probably raise profit margins while keeping the supplier's prices low. If we got close to losing a supplier because of my price pressure, I could always back off so we would both still win.

I was eager to try out the new strategy with a particularly difficult saleswoman from the target group of suppliers. As I rolled out the plan, she took notes and asked questions. Finally, she offered flatly, "I don't think you can do that." My male ego was ruffled as I barked back, "What do you mean I can't do that? As the customer, I can do anything I want." She corrected her statement immediately. "What I should have said," she continued just as if she assumed I knew what she was talking about "is that we cannot legally do what you suggest. It would violate the Reciprocity law." I was dumbfounded, without any idea if she was pulling my leg or telling me something in earnest.

I was trying to negotiate an illegal deal and I ignorantly thought I was doing something clever. Reciprocity is a legal concept involving buying and selling that I should have known. She knew it, and she wasn't a lawyer, either. To attain the professional level, we must know about the law.

The Basics

We need to know more about the Uniform Commercial Code, contract law, and some federal laws. An absolutely essential reference for your professional library is a work of art by two lawyers who were also experienced professional buyers. *The Purchasing Manager's Desk Book of Purchasing Law* is the best authority available. The authors, Donald B. King and James J. Ritterskamp, Jr., and the publisher, Prentice Hall, have created a masterwork of reference for purchasing pros that is written with the buyer in mind. You will find extensive authoritative treatment of legal matters relevant to buyers and sellers. Obtain and study this reference book.

For instance, the section in the book on Reciprocity points out that the threat of coercion implied by trading of purchases and sales in fixed ratios is an attempt to monopolize trade. In the personal case cited above, the risk of consequences was small, but the personal embarrassment was high and my level of professionalism was low. It prompted me to delve into purchasing law and apply much of that acquired knowledge to the art and science of negotiation.

The foundation of purchasing law in the US is the Uniform Commercial Code (UCC). The UCC is not a federal law, but operates similarly in that it applies almost uniformly from state to state. The UCC is a set of laws affecting the purchase and sale, storage, transportation, security, and payment of goods having a value of more than $500. This body of law evolved throughout the 20th century, gaining momentum during the Great Depression years. Our maturing, technologically advanced nation had commercial and security motivations to homogenize the fractious business laws of its economically divergent states. It would be easier for business if one common set of statutes applied across state lines.

Lest you conclude that the UCC is too esoteric, let's take the case of oral contracts. Oral contracts are common and almost everybody has used them, so how does this common custom affect negotiation? Well, if you have invested time and money in establishing your terms and conditions, perhaps a certification program, you have wasted your negotiation efforts. The wisdom of

Sam Goldwyn applies here: "An oral contract isn't worth the paper it's printed on." A frequently heard defense for the oral contract is, "We have always done it this way."

This leads us to the legal principle called conduct of the parties. This states that a contract may be made in any fashion, including conduct of the parties that recognizes such a contract. This means that if we negotiate a deal that calls for shipping of goods on some acceptable schedule, receipt, invoice and payment terms, and we are mutually happy with this deal, great. The problem arises when the process breaks down. Whose terms and conditions apply in this case of default? Do you agree that this is getting messy? We would spend more in legal fees to untangle this mess than we would have in prudent study of purchasing law as it applies to negotiation.

The UCC governs transactions involving goods in virtually the same fashion in 49 of the 50 states; Louisiana being the exception. The Napoleonic civil code, the historic basis for Louisiana's laws, did not and still does not correspond to the prevailing laws in all the other states. Save for that exception, the balance of the country is in accord with the UCC.

The UCC and the law of Contracts specify that the four conditions below must be met for a contract to be formed. This is essential information to the negotiators, be they buyers or sellers. We will examine each for impact on negotiation because they contain much information, almost none of which is obvious.

- Competent parties
- Valid legal subject matter
- Mutual consideration
- Agreement of the parties (offer and acceptance)

"Competent parties" has the usual meanings: age of majority, unduly affected by drugs, alcohol, or dementia. But it has another, more subtle meaning. "Competent parties" also means that buyer and seller have the authority to enter into a contract. We will assume here that the contracting parties are corporations that act through agents to conduct purchase and sale negotiations. An immediate question that should arise is, "Does this person have the authority to negotiate?" The question applies to buyer and seller, but not equally.

Does the average salesperson have the authority to negotiate a contract? The fact is that the generic salesperson or "drummer" has very little authority. They are authorized to solicit orders and take these invitations back to higher corporate powers for approval. Thus the law provides the basis for the negotiation tactic that we call 'Higher Authority.' How about the buyer? Does he or she have the authority? The answer is yes and is the reverse of the seller. It comes as a surprise to most people that the buyers have at least the apparent authority and the sellers do not. But we are not done.

Further complicating this competent-parties issue is the actual authority of the buyer. Many have signature authorities that limit the dollar amounts or types of purchases they may make. If a buyer acts beyond his or her authority level, the deal may be unenforceable against the corporate principal. The buyer who exceeded his or her authority may become personally liable for damages suffered by the principal. The UCC imposes the burden upon the agent to determine the scope of authority the agent with whom they are dealing possesses. As a practical matter, who wants to invest all the time and effort in chasing down an unenforceable deal? Negotiators must establish the authority of the other person before proceeding in any meaningful fashion.

Valid legal subject matter is important because we cannot legally contract for illegal activities. Return to our literary business magnate, the Godfather. Allegedly, Don Corleone issued 'contracts' on others who disagreed with him. These contacts for hits are illegal and unenforceable because the subject matter is illegal. A more mundane example is the agreement of buyer and seller to ship in-state but invoice to the out-of-state office in order to avoid the sales, use, or inventory taxes. Here is a clear example of the professional interplay between you and your lawyer. You perk up at the very suggestion and refer this matter to your lawyer. The legal principle is that parties cannot conspire to violate the rights of the sovereign (state, in this case). Moreover, while tax avoidance is legal, tax evasion is not.

"Mutual consideration" refers to the exchange of value between the parties and is generally not a misunderstood topic. Sometimes parties agree to no-cash consideration such as barter. If you are unfamiliar with the legal or tax consequences, you defer here again to competent legal advice.

"Agreement of the parties" is a far more important matter to those negotiating. It might seem that which party makes an offer and which accepts is of no great consequence. That would be a mistake in the case of the purchase and sale of goods. The UCC says that the Offeror is the master of the offer. In general, the terms and conditions of the Offeror are those that govern the transaction.

A common controversy between buyer and seller is that of whose terms and conditions apply. This tug of war is referred to as the 'Battle of the Forms.' As a practical business matter, you always want to be the Offeror. This settles the battle. Many firms go as far as to print on their Request for Quotation (RFQ) forms the words "This is not an Offer to Buy" so that their RFQ will not be confused with their Purchase Order (PO) forms.

Their PO forms will also contain the words "This is an Offer to Buy" so that the identity of the Offeror is abundantly clear. By the way, in the oral contract case above, where the conduct of the parties created the path of contract, the need to establish Offeror and Offeree is ignored, thereby making any dispute messier. It pays to know and follow the law in negotiations. In this case, the negotiation technique to apply is to be the party that makes the offer, the Offeror, in the negotiation.

The UCC has a variety of provisions with which many purchasing and sales agents are familiar. Some common concepts are liquidated damages, breaches and remedies, delivery, transportation terms, and scores of others. One provision is less familiar and a tad surprising. It is the legal obligation of good faith and honesty of the merchants (buyer and seller) in all dealings. Put another way, honesty in the buy/sell relationship is the law! "Who'da thunk it?" as Yogi Berra might phrase it.

Honesty and Ethics

Honesty and ethics are a source of many jokes in the business world. Commerce's reputation for honesty and integrity is in such a state of disrepair that the laws may not be enforced and as a result are frequently ignored. The moral argument is that we should be doing the right thing whether someone is watching or not. We do not need to moralize. The truth is that honesty in negotiation is just good business.

The UCC states in Section 1-203 that "Every contract or duty within this Act imposes the duty of good faith in its performance or enforcement." The UCC states elsewhere that this obligation for good faith cannot be disclaimed. Other provisions of the UCC include 'Honesty in Fact' and 'Fair Dealing.' Thus, two parties cannot agree to lie, cheat and steal, because it violates the dictates of the sovereign.

One of the effects of the Act as a whole is to mitigate the old doctrine of 'caveat emptor' or 'let the buyer beware.' In its place, it imposes the duty of parties to interact honestly. It also installs some affirmative duties of the parties. A buyer, for instance, cannot take refuge in the claim of ignorance. The law assumes that the buyer is an expert at the bargaining table and imposes upon the buyer the duty to use its professional abilities to the fullest extent. This means that a buyer is presumed to know what any buyer of similar station would know if he made reasonable investigation that any professional buyer would make under the circumstances.

So far, we have covered the legal requirement for honesty, although we noted that ethical behavior is also required. Well, what is ethical? One distinction is that the law is the lowest form of ethics. Ethics, therefore, is a cut above what is minimally legal and conforms to higher standards of behavior. It follows logically that one cannot possibly act ethically if one does not know what is legal. This confusion is due to our pop culture. When some politician is being led off in cuffs, still mugging for the camera, the standard sound bite is, "I did nothing wrong!" Well, by 'wrong', that politico probably means illegal, which is in some doubt. Almost without doubt, they are not concerned with what is ethical. We can consider something to be wrong if it falls below our ethical limits, even though it is legal. Divulging a competitor's price is an example. It might not illegal to do so, but it would be unethical for most buyers. Moreover, what is to be gained that could not be reached by ethical means? We will come back to this question after our discussion of applicable federal laws.

For more extensive information on ethical practices, including sample ethics policies, refer to the country's two leading authorities on the practice of professional purchasing, the Institute of Supply Management (formerly the National Association of Purchasing Management) at www.ism.ws or the American Purchasing Society at www.american-purchasing.com.

Federal Laws

Federal laws can have a huge effect on negotiations. If we trade overseas, we have probably come across the Foreign Corrupt Trade Practices Act and the Convention for the International Sale of Goods. Coupled with customs regulations, import and export laws, and a plethora of other issues, this is an area in which you want to seek liberal amounts legal help.

Much of the Clayton Act has been amended by the Robinson-Patman Act except for the provision concerning restraint of trade. For instance, be wary of negotiating a deal with a supplier that limits your or his ability to deal with competitors. The Sherman Antitrust Act encompasses the reciprocity concerns we previously cited as well as monopolies. Bundling of services may also run afoul of anti-monopoly statues, so it is wise and prudent to seek legal assistance with these matters.

Robinson-Patman Act

The law of single greatest effect on buyers and sellers in negotiation is the Robinson-Patman law. This is the statute with which we will have the greatest daily contact and be exposed to the most danger. It concerns discrimination in pricing. One of its consequences is that the law makes it illegal for buyers to knowingly induce or receive discriminatory prices. Buyers violate the law when they place orders at prices that they know (and in some cases, should have known) are exceptionally low and/or below the supplier's costs. Exceptions are made for private label products, loss leaders, matching of competitor's prices in good faith, and other reasons. Lawyers expert in purchasing matters counsel buyers to obtain cost justification for the prices and proof that other customers are offered these prices on proportionally equal terms. We care most about the cost justification provision, as the issue of price comes up in virtually every negotiation.

"Where do I have to be?"

In Chapter 2, we identified the most important tool of the trade as Cost Analysis. Legal cost-justification for a price is obtained through the negotiating tool of Cost Analysis. We also noted in Chapter 2 that the most popularly cited method of establishing price was the cost-plus method. All of these concepts are related and form a seamless process. This is why we devoted two chapters of this book to preparation.

No matter all of this preparation and knowledge of the law, the markets, communication skills and negotiation techniques, the climax culminates in the form of this legendary question, "Where do I have to be?" Every buyer has heard this query numerous times.

When pressed to disclose their answers in safe "theoretical" discussions, buyers admit to a variety of evasive answers. They indicate a range, a target, and even a hard number. Probed further, they confess to exaggerating the figure a bit, in anticipation of and to offset the expected lie of the other side. To paraphrase the warden in Cool Hand Luke, "What we have here is a commercial case of liar's poker."

This question is in reality a trap set to expose the price centered purchasing negotiator. Not only are the above cited answers unethical, the dishonesty may be illegal, and most importantly we have violated everything we know about cost-centered negotiation. Any of these "theoretical" answers marks us as amateurs who understand little of the TCO basis of negotiation.

This pervasive question presents an ideal opportunity to parse our answer in detail and relate the words to the tools, techniques, communication skills, and practical legal considerations we have acquired. We will set up a table after the answer below to identify the relevant negotiation tool or technique and practical legal consideration.

In the negotiation setting, given the strictures of Robinson-Patman, our passion for the Best Value (lowest TCO) and our professional dexterity at avoiding traps, we have a ready and effective answer to the supplier's question of "Where do I have to be?" The answer is:

> *"Mister or Madam Supplier, let me be certain that I understand what is being asked. Did I understand correctly that I am to decide your price? If so, I cannot tell you what your price should be for several reasons important to us. (I am sure that) Neither of us wishes to run afoul of Robinson-Patman provisions. More importantly, to preserve our relationship and because of the importance of the issues, we need to look at the TCO, not just the price. Since I heard that the price is a function of the cost, why don't we look first at the price, then into the costs? I am most interested in the best value, which we define as the lowest TCO. Would you be willing to work this way?"*

This answer assimilates our skills in many of the scattered disciplines and ties the process together in a way that reinforces our TCO and Win-Win message. It is also completely honest. We are interested in TCO. If we can eliminate some costs and thereby reduce the price in the process, so much the better.

The words we use complement our Win-Win strategy. The constant deflection of price to cost reinforces the TCO significance to which the supplier may not be fully attuned. As a professional in procurement, you will never go wrong with costs. Seize every opportunity to bring the negotiation around to cost matters. The suppliers will come to realize that your goal of lowest TCO drives the negotiation process, not ego, price, or other hidden agendas that alienate the parties.

As a reminder, tools are Cost and Price analysis, techniques and communication chapters are recited in Chapter 6, and practical legal considerations are as presented in this chapter.

Words	Negotiation Tool/ Technique or Practical Legal Consideration
Let me be certain that I understand what is being asked.	'I' statement, reflective response
Did I understand correctly that I am to decide your price?	'I' statement, reflective response
If so, I cannot tell you what your price should be for several reasons important to us.	'I' statement, TCO, Price Analysis, Cost Analysis
(I am sure that) Neither of us wishes to run afoul of Robinson-Patman provisions.	(implied) 'I' statement, Robinson-Patman,
More importantly, to preserve our relationship and because of the importance of the issues, we need to look at the TCO, not just the price.	Win-Win strategy by stressing issue and relationship, TCO
Since I heard that the price is a function of the cost...	'I' statement, reflective response
Why don't we look first at the price, then into the costs?	'I' statement modified with first person pronoun 'we' to bring the sides together, Price Analysis, Cost Analysis
I am most interested in the best value, which we define as the lowest TCO.	TCO, TCO
Would you be willing to work this way?"	'You" statement intended to inspire a 'yes' or 'yes' response

The 'Where do I have to be' question also spotlights the practical, ethical, and legal implications that can occur when we lose track of costs and exhibit poor negotiation behavior. Let's examine the alternative, some would say normal, buyer's response to the supplier's question. Suppose we are price-focused folks who do not prepare for our negotiations and have little formal study or training in our craft. Unwilling to concern ourselves with the trifling qualities of ethics and honesty, we invite our supplier to a pick-pocket session. We pretend to listen to their offer, biding our time until we hear that magical question signaling that the supplier is finally ready to get down to business.

We have three possible responses to that question: the target, the range, and a percentage. The range and the percentage are really higher mathematics forms of the target, requiring either assumption or calculation to arrive at the low end of the range or percentage. This low end becomes the target, so all three answers have the same effect. No doubt, we have gilded the lily a bit so that the target is actually low-balled. This low number, we justify, is our HID. We spring into action, announcing with unabashed ignorance, "You'll have to be at least 10% lower to get the deal."

What are the practical, ethical, and legal considerations posed by this answer? As a practical matter, suppose that this particular seller knows well our price driven mentality and has factored in a fifteen percent price inflation to protect against our expected low ball offer. The seller resists the urge to jump over the desk, give you a big kiss and hug and say, "It's a deal – and to think that I was prepared to go to all the way to 15 percent." Versed in negotiation, the supplier knows not to accept the offer. Otherwise, it will appear that the seller places no value on price and invite further reduction attempts. Instead, the seller bargains a little more, trying to increase the dollar amount of the sale or wrangle some other favorable terms. Finally, the supplier reluctantly agrees, congratulating the buyer on his tough tactics and great deal. Politely, the supplier waits until she is safely back at her office before allowing herself to yuck it up with the sales manager about how they nailed you again.

From an ethics viewpoint, the buyer lied. Is lying unethical? Worse yet, the buyer derived no advantage by his dishonest act. Lying for financial gain might be understandable, but lying to pay more has to qualify for adoption by acclamation into the Business Dummies Hall of Fame.

If we are not shamed and embarrassed by the potential for practical and ethical consequences, the legal implications should be enough to pay close attention. A landmark case in 1971 found a buyer personally and his employer company corporately to be liable for damages due to lying about the prices. The net result of the low-balling lies was to force, induce, or receive discriminatory prices in violation of Robinson-Patman and other commercial statutes. The courts absolved the supplier of any wrongdoing, believing that the supplier had acted in good faith in meeting competitive prices. The court rejected explanations from the buyer and the employer about "being placed in peril whenever ... engaged in hard bargaining." The court noted that it was not the hard bargaining that controlled the matter, but the misrepresentation of the prices that created the liability.

Well, that is quite a revelation. We see that our resort to honesty, Cost and Price Analysis, and good negotiation techniques obtain far better results all around than the illegal, unethical, and backfired practicality of these ignoble alternatives. This is one more example of how we will never go wrong by sticking with the costs.

Consulting Your Attorney

Finally, we return to the reason that it is wise to know when to consult an attorney. In general, the right time is before anything bad happens. Think of this principle as preventive medicine, except this is prevention of outrageous legal costs after the fact. Keep your lawyer in the loop early on and save yourself a lot of money later.

Consider these two examples of how the need to consult a lawyer might not be an obvious choice. For legal definition purposes, what are goods? A trick question, you say. No, a legal question, but the two may be the same thing. Goods are defined in the UCC as things and are differentiated from real property, land and buildings. Interpretations of the law create precedents and case law which are no matters for pretenders. One of the interpretations of the UCC is that goods must be moveable at the time of sale. Minerals that are to be removed from the land are considered goods if they are to be severed from the land by the seller. The reasoning is that if the minerals were removed by the buyer, any contract involving the minerals would be governed by real estate laws, not the UCC.

In an example regarding warranties, a fertile ground for legal disputes, a case involving cardiac surgery came under the auspices of the UCC. While heart surgery would seem to be a service and not goods, the estate of the decedent sued the medical team, hospital and others under the warranty protections afforded by the UCC. The decedent's estate contended that by removing the heart and blood from the body and cooling them down to facilitate the introduction of anti-rejection drugs, oxygen, and other pharmaceuticals, the medical team had effectively transformed the blood into 'goods.' As goods, they were entitled to the UCC warranty protection of fitness for its particular purpose.

The moral of the story is one we have already acknowledged: No one is as smart as they look. Resolve any doubts in favor of consulting the attorney. Even when you feel on solid ground, periodic review of your business processes by competent counsel is always a wise plan.

Summary

A deficiency in knowledge of commercial law is among the greatest faults of purchasing professionals. This deficiency affects our negotiation efforts in the areas of UCC, federal laws, and contract law. Negotiators schooled in the basics of commercial law are an asset to legal consultants and a boost to the negotiation process.

Ethics and good faith are requirements imposed by law by the UCC. The law also exacts different standards of buyer and seller conduct. Moreover, statutes and interpretations of them create a negotiation landscape. The importance of being the Offeror is that our terms and conditions apply.

Federal laws forbid inducing or receiving discriminatory prices. Driving a supplier below costs has its own practical, ethical, and legal considerations. Instead, we are far better off to deploy communication skills and negotiation techniques in tandem with Price and Cost Analysis.

Consultation with lawyers is best accomplished early in the process, periodically for prevention's sake, and whenever the purchasing pro identifies or senses legal peril.

Chapter 9

Tactics and Counter-Tactics

At last, we arrive at the point where many folks involved in negotiation think is all that matters - tactics and counter tactics. Tactics are to negotiation what knives are to cooking. It is easy to pick them up, use them, and with no practice at all be instantly capable of hurting anyone in range, especially ourselves. The truth is that knowing how to use them makes us only marginally better cooks and negotiators. We do, however, loom as formidable parties to be feared and respected; we look like we know what we are doing. Whether we use these tools to become masters of our craft or just wield them in a frantic display of confusion is a choice that distinguishes the pretender from the professional.

We obsess so much over tactics because they are glorious, the object of praise and celebration in movies and legend. The good guy/bad guy gambit is familiar to anyone who ever watched a cop show. Books by famous egomaniacs would have the reader believe that fortunes of the kingdoms rested on the monarch's skill at negotiation tactics. It just isn't so. Dedication to preparation, advanced communication skills, and ability with other tools (Price Analysis, Cost Analysis, Supplier Certification, etc.) distinguish the successful negotiator.

The allure of tactics stems from their association with the face-to-face confrontations. This is arguably the most intriguing mystique of negotiation. It is certainly more exciting than Cost Analysis or

Robinson-Patman. Typically, those excited by the hunt and the kill are the T-Rex, Win-Lose folks we identified in Chapter 5. The selection and application of tactics should complement and epitomize the negotiation process.

Recall that we estimated the amount of face-to-face time in negotiation as a fraction of the total, amounting to between 5 and 10 percent. It is this small slice of our efforts, however, in which tactics exert the greatest influence. That is, mastery of tactics can disproportionately affect the outcome of the negotiation. Incompetence in the use of tactics can outweigh any other tactical advantage.

Another bona fide reason for knowing all about tactics is that we want to recognize them when they are used on us. The old military adage notes that a tactic recognized is a tactic neutralized. It is helpful to think of tactics as the language of negotiation. Our goal is to make certain that tactics are not a foreign language to us.

Mastery of tactics allows the skilled negotiator to choose the best one for the job. Good guy/bad guy would probably be inappropriate in a Win-Win strategy involving long-term, successful relationships built upon lowest TCO. Similarly, the Cost Analysis tool is fairly useless in a Win-Lose adversarial strategy.

Our choice of tactics will be determined by the preparation, strategy, communication, and interpersonal factors that have shaped the negotiation process. An example of such an influence is the High Initial Demand (HID). HID is borne of the human-nature imperative to do better. An asking price higher than the 'must have' position is an offset to the expected demand to do better. We choose and deploy various tactics that we believe will stimulate or guide desired behavior.

The rationale behind using tactics at all is one of caution. Except in vary rare cases, we cannot fully trust the other side. Trust, like credit, must be earned. Only a fool would extend credit to a stranger. Trust is merely a form of credit. Therefore, we test for traps cautiously.

We also truly do not know what the other party wants. We probe with questions and make intelligence estimates of what we think their issues will be, their HID, 'nice to have,' and 'must have' positions. Couple the fact of the cautious need to defend from aggression with our ignorance of the other side, and we see that the need for tactics will always exist.

No single set of tactics is the best to use. Circumstances will govern their use, so we cannot learn the 'top ten' list and discard the rest. The best tactics are those that advance our strategy. A harmony of message and messenger imparts an aura of professionalism that smoothes out the rough spots and makes the experience more enjoyable.

For organizational purposes, we classify our most popular negotiation tactics into four main categories: Maneuvers, Flyers, Gambits and Ruses. These range from the noble to the not-so-noble and will appear unpredictably throughout the negotiation process. While the other party may use these tactics indiscriminately, or as they find them effective, we want to be certain that we align the tactic to suit our strategy. Examples will make clear how we can do this consistently.

Maneuvers

The **Maneuvers** include:

- Higher Authority
- Split the Difference
- Trading Concessions
- No Statement

We know about **Higher Authority** from our legal discussion in Chapter 8 and that it is our duty to establish the authority of the seller in advance of any meaningful talks. Yet it happens that the seller extracts our best offer and then claims that she must check with the manager and get back to us. What should we do in the jaws of this trap? Immediately suspend the talks by saying, "Oh, I did not realize that you did not have the authority to make this deal. Everything is off the table now, because we might be guilty of bargaining in bad faith and we don't want to do that. I tell you what. Get your boss down here today and we'll try to wrap this up. Otherwise, we may have to make entirely alternate plans." If the seller's tactic was an honest mistake, she stands aware of the problem. If not, the tactic has been exposed and a warning issued for future dealings. The best route is to avoid the trap by qualifying the authority beforehand.

Who has not used the **Split the Difference** maneuver? It seems honest and innocent enough, and often it is. It has powerful impact in the hands of the artful because they know that only one out an infinite number of possible splits are 50/50. You never want to be the first to offer to split the difference. It transfers veto power to the other side and may worsen your position. This is another of those actions that confuses the other side, much like a seller conceding price reductions in successively increasing amounts. Instead, get the other guy to offer to split the difference. Here is one painful example. I once had a customer who bemoaned the fact that we were so close, and how he hated to see the deal fall apart. He walked me down the aisle, extolling the virtue of our work together and how badly he felt about not being able to accept what he knew to be a fair offer from me, but the budget was under-funded. In a misguided gesture of conciliation and without getting conditional agreement first, I offered to split the difference. The next day, he told me that he had considered my offer, but still could not go along, but we were so close. I offered to split it again, to which he reluctantly agreed. Doing the math, he gave 25% and I gave 75% in this 'split'.

The **Trading Concession** is a very seductive maneuver. It seems entirely justified that one good turn deserves another. The complication is the perceived value stumbling block that we discussed in Chapter 3. You need not reciprocate with a concession for every one you earn, because you do not know the actual value to the other side. Gift certificates provide an excellent example. Merchants love to sell these because they are priced at retail, they bring customers back, and they have a low rate of redemption. As part of a settlement negotiation with an unhappy customer, gift certificates are a common concession. The customer may never use it, but it satisfies the demand that the "You owe me" debt be paid off. Thus merchants concede a high perceived value item at a low actual cost. Many skilled negotiators build in concessions of little actual value into their negotiation plan. This is a good idea, as is the related concept of planning to lose on some battles.

The **No Statement** is a big tactic with a little name, and it packs all the potency of Napoleon. Powerful in itself, its seeds spread over a field of equally effective tactics. Faced with "No" for an answer, we can ignore it, react angrily, accept it without challenge, ask for more information, or react with some combination. All have merit for different reasons, making this tactic one of the most common in negotiation. Sales pros tend to simply ignore the 'No' statement. In some cases, it seems that they have grown a membrane in their inner ear so that every time the word 'No' forms on the buyer's lips, it is immediately interpreted as 'Maybe.' Everyone involved in negotiations would do well to emulate such wisdom. 'No' is nothing more than an opening position.

In Chapter 6, we scrutinized the technique of neither agreeing nor disagreeing. As a counter to the 'No' statement, we apply this technique. We are interested in learning more about what motivates the 'No' position. Now is a perfect time to promote elaboration by invoking the "Tell me about it" technique. The announcement was intended to claim certain inviolable territory, but the assertion may be in earnest or a form of posturing. In either event, we want to determine what motivates the statement. Suppose your counterpart states, "We can negotiate anything but delivery in less than 6 weeks." Doesn't this strike you as curious? An immediate reaction is to discover exactly what this time limitation means and why it is put into play on the first pitch. It could indicate that orders are backed up for production but that advancement to the head of the line could be arranged if we pay additional freight and a convenience fee to bump down some other orders already in place. It could also mean that the advance time cannot be compressed by any method whatsoever. Perhaps it is even a High Initial Demand designed to flush out our reaction and thereby gauge our 'must have' position. Any response but the flat invitation to expound on the position by telling us more about it falls into one or more traps.

Non-negotiable positions are one of the seeds of the 'No' statement that grow to take on a significance of their own. An aggressive proclamation of boundary limits warns everyone that the very mention of certain topics will not be tolerated. Is this a bullying tactic? Maybe, or it could be borne from a feeling of inadequacy. This person is fearful and probably doubts his ability to handle the negotiation in a more subtle manner. This is our signal to approach this person in the personality style they find most suitable. Doing so lowers the communication barriers for your counterpart and helps them to express themselves after overcoming the initial terror.

Here is one example of how the result is better for both parties when an earnest application of the non-negotiable position is clarified by learning the underlying motivation. The seller says that the price is fixed and not up for discussion. Well, that 'No' statement bounces off our ears and excites our 'maybe' bone. Why is the price fixed? If the quality, service, or delivery parameters change, wouldn't the price change to reflect the shuffled cost constituents? Of course they would, in any logical set of circumstances. If the seller is envisioning a one-shot deal and you have more extensive quantities in mind, the price won't be fixed for very long into the discussion.

Another related tactic is to introduce a host of non-negotiable demands, many of the straw or red herring variety. The purpose of this 'No' statement overload is to withdraw these later in exchange for the elimination or reduction of more legitimate demands of the other side. This is often an effective tactic. To counter it, keep a supply of your own non-negotiable items ready to insert in the talks. Your efforts at being reasonable by keeping your non-negotiables off the table may not work in the face of unreasonable demands from the other side. Expect this tactic more often in Win-Lose strategies.

The Flyers

As we move to Flyers, we can expect these to pop up at almost anytime under any strategy. The **Flyers** include:

- The Flinch
- The Hot Potato
- The Do Better
- Silence

A **Flinch** is a visible reaction that portrays an emotional message. As a boy at camp, I enjoyed long gun training. The trick to pull on a new kid was to have him watch the older guys absorb the recoil from shooting 12-gauge shotguns, and then give the tender foot an unloaded weapon. When the trigger clicked, the new guy flinched back in nervous expectation of the explosion reaction he had just witnessed. Business people too are conditioned to anticipate reactions. As a negotiation tactic, buyers often flinch to show displeasure with a seller's proposal. A particularly effective occasion to practice your flinch is in the price increase negotiation. Price increases are not high up on the favorites list for sales people to do with their customers. It is stressful and unpleasant. Accordingly, many prefer to announce the price increase by impersonal letter. If the price increase is a problem, don't let them get away with it without a face-to-face meeting. Summon your dumbness, and call them, expressing an urgent invitation to visit with you in person and explain their cost justification. Allow the person to go through his or her entire presentation. Wear a look of amazement on your face before reacting with a jaw drop, or a stunned look, or some other gesture of disbelief. Even though the salesperson may know you are overplaying the part, the discomfort may stimulate some concessionary talk. The price increase is often not fully justified, so the seller is looking for your reaction to judge how to proceed. Coupled with other tools we have in our tool kit, we may be able to roll back the unjustified portion.

This brings us to another off-shoot tactic of the 'No' statement that we call the **Hot Potato**. This is a very effective tactic, particularly in the hands of sophisticated buyers. A buyer may say to a seller, "In our business, quality, service, and delivery are givens. You wouldn't be sitting here if you didn't clear these hurdles. So, it really all comes down to price." If the seller accepts that tactic, and agrees that it just comes down to price, wow! What a score for the buyer. In one fluid motion, the Hot Potato was buttered up, served, and swallowed whole. It is a clever way to minimize and freeze all other cost components but price while congratulating the seller on its admission into this elite class of lowest TCO, where only its price matters. Remember that not all of our negotiations will be Win-Win, and that this tactic may be better suited for the Win-Lose strategy. In order to counter this Hot Potato, a seller must recognize it, reject it, and return the talk to cost components. Is the buyer entertaining a low-price competitor because she feels the low price is on the street? If so, the seller may be able to lower his price in return for other concessions. If the buyer is not interested in TCO, better to know early on so the seller may adjust his negotiation strategy to suit the buyer. The buyer or seller must challenge the Hot Potato as soon as it appears.

The **Do Better** tactic has been an accepted part of life since grade school. When faced with the ultimatum that one must do better, the conditioned response is to just do it. It reminds us of that cross second-grade teacher who caught us with sloppy, incomplete homework. A casual remark in response to a supplier's question could be, "You'll have to do better." This rather open-ended comment could apply to price, quality, delivery, and service, or it could be an expression of disbelief. It often spurs a bettering of the offer or a helpful explanation, as was the case with our homework. Skilled sales pros may counter with the question, "How much better?" This response is another Broadway opening to launch into our Price Analysis and Cost Analysis investigations, much as we did in the case of the "Where do I have to be" question.

The **Silence** tactic is intimately and explicitly understood as a personal relationship tool between men and women. Leaving that field to the experts, we will move on to the business applications. Silence is unique for its absence of words. Unless we add body language, this tactic is completely open to subjective interpretation. I learned the power of the tactic quite by accident. In a routine sales visit, the VP accompanying the National Accounts rep assigned to me summarily took over the meeting and proceeded to dazzle me with an unexpected proposal for a new product. He told me about its markets, the features and benefits, and how it would supplement our current business. I sat in amazement and a bit of amusement as this fellow sped through his presentation and brushed aside signals of his prospect's confusion. His mission was to get to the closing question. As he raced to the climax of his spiel, he ended unexpectedly on the price.

I was so taken aback that I was not sure what was next. As I remained silent, his facial expression betrayed fear and embarrassment. He had ended on the price. My silence must in some way reflect my disquiet with the price. After an uncomfortable eternity of 15 seconds or so, he couldn't stand it. His next uttering improved the price. He was negotiating with himself! Since this tactic is silence, enough said.

The Gambits

The next set of tactics is Gambits. The word derives from the slang Italian expression for tripping someone. The use of Gambits implies a more cautious approach where we raise the alert level and actively guard against traps that might be set for us, wittingly or innocently. **Gambits** include:

- Good Guy / Bad Guy
- The Invalid Offer
- The Lesser of Two Evils
- Sacred Writings

The **Good Guy / Bad Guy** tactic is arguably the most barefaced. Virtually everyone has used it or has been abused by it. Should we then be ashamed to use it? Heck, no. We use it because it works. Everyone with whom I have ever done business or discussed negotiation has a favorite story about this tactic. Many involve car salesmen. The common thread in all situations is that neither guy is on your side, no matter what it may seem under the individual circumstances. Counter this trite tactic by exposing it. If the bad guy is the one in higher authority, definitely get him out from behind the curtain. Like the Wizard of Oz, he won't seem so omnipotent without his visual aid. Don't fall for the trap of negotiating with one or the other. Declare that you will treat them as one voice and demand that they caucus on who has the authority, or else ask for a third party.

The **Invalid Offer** is sometimes associated with shady hit-and-run, high-pressure sales routines. It is frequently coupled with the ticking clock gambit wherein you must buy within a short and immediate time frame. It enjoys popularity in the case of impulse purchases like time-share vacation property. If you exhibit the temerity of taking the time to think over a proposed fast-spoken deal, your penalty is exacted in the form of a higher price. Faced with that insult, the potential buyer immediately demands the original price and the noose is cinched. The tactic of withdrawing the offer simply reinforced the value of the time-limitation gambit. By 'allowing' you to buy at the withdrawn offer price, the seller appears to be making a concession, thereby increasing the value of the purchase. The best way to counter the tactic is to avoid impulse purchases because you have no preparation time. Recognizing the tactic for what it is will sometimes cause the seller to drop its use.

The **Lesser of Two Evils** is so subtle a tactic that it hides in a niceness disguise. It happens when the sales clerk says, "Cash or credit," and it also happens when the salesman says, "Would you like to arrange the freight or use our carrier?" In sales, this closing technique is so important it has more than one name. Two are the Presumptive Close and the Theory of Many Little Yeses. The theory presumes that an affirmative decision has already been made to buy, thus psychologically foreclosing doubt on the buyer's part. A seller never wants to arm the customer with objections, so a question is phrased in a fashion that has only affirmative responses. We are not responsible for other people's phraseology, so we redirect the conversation. To counter this tactic, we clearly indicate that we have other choices. Something like this will suffice: "Oh, did I give you the impression that we had come to a meeting of the minds? Well, let's see if we can clear things up before we go any further." The rejoinder serves notice that closing techniques not devoted to lowering costs need not be applied.

One of my favorite tactics is **Sacred Writings**. It is so effective because of the persuasive suggestion of the written word. We believe what we read, even the jaded, skeptical purchasing types. In a cab from midtown Atlanta to the airport, I read a national newspaper. On the front page was a picture and obituary of a Supreme Court justice. This judge had retired in my college years, and I could not remember if I favored or opposed his politics, but another piece of my life had slipped away. I ruminated sadly on his passing. The very next morning, in my hotel room, I picked up the same national paper and found a picture in the errata section. It was the correct old dead judge. Nonetheless, I had firmly believed what I had read.

Supplier Certification programs serve this same subliminal purpose in the purchase and sale negotiation. If a supplier does not meet the minimum written standards, what is the conclusion reached? Two logical choices are that there is no use trying or that it takes major concessions in some elements of cost to offset its short comings. If the TCO is too high, the supplier should be discouraged and the tactic has been effective. If the result of the tactic is to reduce the TCO, then the tactic has succeeded. The written standards disqualify a supplier to the extent that the customer is willing to enforce them. In any event, the message springs from the use of Sacred Writings.

The Ruses

The Ruses comprise tactics ranging from wild to tame and are to be used judiciously. If you spot these, regard them with suspicion. The other negotiator may be adroitly deploying or clumsily utilizing these. The **Ruses** include:

- The Head Fake
- The Straws
- Funnie Munnie
- Madman Mania
- The Walk
- Artful Anger
- Self Control
- Puppy Dog Pose

The **Head Fake** is the introduction of a phony issue or position for the purpose of concealing the real ones. This tactic pops up frequently in Win-Lose strategies, labor negotiations, and settlement talks between estranged parties. The head faker has little interest in honesty or much concern with how the other side does in the negotiation. You can recognize the tactic or at least be cautious when a point that you did not expect enters the discussion. It could be legitimate, so investigate with open-ended questions and requests to tell you more about it. Typically, the drive for the decoy will later incorporate the real issue, which will be associated in some way to make the real issue seem less important.

The **Straws** are red herring issues. They have little value to the other side or to us and are placed on the table for their value as concessions later. The non-negotiables tactic we raised earlier often falls into this category. A clue to the straw's presence is the introduction of unanticipated terms and conditions.

Whenever unexpected data appear, be alert to the possibility that the information has marginal value.

Funnie Munnie is a truly clumsy tactic. It involves the expression of a price in relative terms that deemphasize cost and try to shame the buyer. "Can you afford 20 cents per day to protect your family?" How about, "Make just four easy payments of $39.95?" These paraphrased TV quotes take aim at pride and responsibility. "Why, of course I can afford that, I do care about these things, and here's the money to prove it," is the response the ads intend to provoke. Price quotations for leasing big-ticket items provide a notorious example: $1.71 per passenger revenue passenger mile per hour per operating year assuming 85% seat occupancy and a 10-year life with normal maintenance costs. What does this mean? It states an incomprehensible set of facts and offers insufficient information with which to make any calculation. Get the Funnie Munnie translated to dollars and cents in a hurry.

Madman Mania covers a variety of behaviors, usually unsavory, that betray a low skill level in negotiation. People use them because they are effective. Bullies have learned that their antisocial rants help them get their way. They apply that pattern to negotiation as well. Suppose you are dealing with a foul-mouthed, arrogant, abusive egomaniac that has body odor and halitosis - and those are his good points. He rules by a reign of terror and people fear his reputation. The question to ask ourselves is, "So what?" We are not considering a marriage proposal, just a business deal. Bullies do not favor being challenged, and might react angrily when confronted. So what? Stand your ground, rely on your skills, and attend to business. The bully will develop a new, if grudging sense of respect for you, even if he is not sure why.

The **Walk** is one of those tactics that people like to talk about in awe. I once heard a fellow in Dallas refer to his boss in reverent tones. "You should have seen how he handled it. The supplier flew down from Chicago with a team of three, and my boss set the whole thing up. Soon into the meeting, he told them that if his price terms weren't met, they could fly back to Chicago. And then he walked out, giving them ten minutes to decide." Well, it might have just been a high-stakes game of chicken, or maybe it was an effective ploy. In any case, beware of using it in any meaningful way. TCO had no weight in this setting and the relationship did not seem to matter much. These two distinct markings identify the type of negotiator and strategy that he had chosen. If someone walks out on us, what options has our preparation primed us for? Do we need this supplier? Was this supposed to be a Win-Win deal? What is our 'walk away' position? Preparation is the only counter to this tactic.

Artful Anger is a pretty slick trick. Use it sparingly and it works well. Use it too much and lose the deal. Anger is often part of negotiation as frustration boils over. Personality disputes, risks, and stress can flare up in angry outbursts. When someone blows hot and hard, it is probably not personally directed but arises from the general stress of the negotiation process. The tactic appears when the exhibition of anger is art and not science, feigned versus real. We may not know the difference between the real and fake variety, so the treatment is the same. Try not to recoil or change your actions because that would be a signal that the tactic has taken effect. It is not our fault if the other party chooses to lose its mind and act out of anger. Do not change your position or your attitude, but be firm and resolute. This advice may sound similar to that prescribed for dealing with childish temper tantrums, and indeed it is almost the same. If you choose this tactic, use it to counter a case of Madman Mania.

All of these heavy human influences lead us to the **Self Control** tactic. This is an extremely important tactic to master and it is not an easy thing to do. Recall the Godfather's advice about, "It's just business, nothing personal." Isn't that true in negotiation? We have no excuse for losing self control. The justification most often cited is that, "He made me so mad." Horse feathers! This puts the other guy in control. No one can make you mad; you have to let him or her do it to you.

If someone can drive you to an emotional reaction, he can manipulate you and control you. Anger clouds judgment. Why would you ever give that much control to a perfect stranger?

The **Puppy Dog Close** is a sales technique. So is the closing, "Money-back guarantee." Both put the product into your hands so that you have no reason to keep looking. Besides, you really want the product and you have no risk, so why not just take it with you. Did you ever take children to see new puppies? The cute furballs cock their heads in a forlorn pose. The clerk assures you that you can bring the puppy back if your kids don't like it. You correctly estimate two chances of that happening, and Slim is in Lubbock indefinitely.

Power

No discussion of tactics is complete without duly noting the amorphous concept of Power. **Power** does not fit neatly in any maneuver classification because it pervades the entire process. Most authoritative sources on the generic matter of negotiation refer to the three essentials of negotiation as power, time, and information. Our treatment of the purchase-and-sale negotiation takes a different approach than these generic alternatives. We devoted much effort to the preparation stage, involving extensive information gathering and analysis tools. This business treatment of information largely isolates and minimizes the time factor. While time and information are quantifiable commodities, power is far more elusive. Thus we have preserved it for separate treatment.

The intangible notion of power intrigues us. Our definition for negotiation purposes is the ability to say no and to live with the result. This is not the same as tact. Tact is the ability to tell the other guy to go to blazes and to make him look forward to the journey. Power has many different manifestations but one common quality. That quality is perception. Power resides in the perception of the parties.

How would you answer this question? "Who has more power in buy/sell settings?" Virtually always, the immediate response from buyer and seller alike is, "The buyer." If so, let me pose this follow-up: "Well, why then should we bother negotiating with them if we have all this power?"

Nothing is standard about the "standard contract form," yet otherwise sophisticated business folks fall for this tactic in droves. So called standard agreements act as biblical papyrus. The biggest impediment to modifying a standard contract form is the person in the mirror. Start-up businesses often can back themselves into a corner by thinking that they must have a certain deal or contract. An analogous feeling of resignation arises in the banking customer. Remember those buyers who claimed power in buy/sell settings? Curiously, they readily cede the perception and thus the reality of that power to the bank in a mortgage relationship. Banks understand and respect power, so they project that image. Their preprinted forms are a tactic to reinforce the image.

Some years ago, my wife and I restructured our real estate program. In dealing with the bank, we encountered the customary paperwork delay. I am certain many financial institutions plan the delay, then work to convince customer of the bank's willingness to bend over backwards. In retail banking, many customers feel the crush of overwhelming odds, so they don't even question the reams of legal forms set before them at a closing.

At our closing for a small refinance mortgage, the bank presented a preprinted form requiring advance escrow deposits for taxes and insurance. The bank's attorney at the closing insisted the form could not be changed. This tactic might be called nibbling, because it is a faint attempt to bite off a sweeter deal. My retort was that we eliminate the form since I planned to pay the amounts directly when they fell due, not a year in advance so that the bank had my money interest-free. Upon returning to the closing, the attorney had another preprinted form that bumped the rate up a fractional percentage to compensate for the bank's 'loss' of value. I informed the attorney that my patience was exhausted and that I was prepared to forsake the mortgage entirely unless the substitution of terms contrary to those agreed was halted. The balance of the closing went through quite smoothly, with no further power plays on the bank's part.

My walk-away position was that I did not need the bank. I had the ability to go without the mortgage, although I would have preferred to have the cash for available capital. Absent the perception, the emperor had no clothes. The bank makes money when it sells loans. When called on its obvious attempt to fatten its purse, the bank recanted. Call a foul when you see one.

Power has a migratory quality; if you think that you have it, you have it. If you think that they have it, they have it. Do not assume that the other guy has more power. A buyer negotiating with a large company may feel powerless. In that case, he is. But Rule 2 tells us that buyer and seller do not want the same thing. In our capitalist system, each party has power over what it owns. If the other party wants what we have, the stage for negotiation is set. A large seller may have motivations independent of the small volume to be gained in the sale at hand. Consider power to be audacity, confidence, or just a mastery of the process.

Another manifestation of power is reluctance. The aphorism is, "He who wants it most loses." If you want it bad, expect to get it bad. Ironically, power flows in the direction of the party that wants the deal least. This is the basis for the reluctant buyer tactic. I discovered this tactic quite by accident. I had a peculiar client for many years. We were not personally close, but the work and the billings were rewarding. He would call at the last minute and make outrageous demands such as traveling overseas with about a week's notice. On one important occasion, I had prior binding commitments. My refusal was not a tactical response, but a candid statement of regret. I feared riling this fellow because of the relationship and future potential. He persisted to the extent of sweetening the compensation. It made sense to me to consider rescheduling the other commitments. I made a concerted effort, offered concessions to other clients to get the time slots, and learned a valuable lesson about negotiation.

Summary

Tactics are the props players use in the negotiation stage. By themselves, these props cannot compensate for a poor script (negotiation plan) or inadequate study of their parts by the players. Rather, tactics advance the negotiation plan toward the achievement of the strategy.

Accordingly, some tactics are more appropriate to some strategies than others. Our selection of tactics is complemented by the tools and techniques of negotiation. Even though we may not choose to deploy some of the tactics, others may choose to use them. Our ability to recognize tactics equates to our ability to counter them.

Appendices

Appendix A

In order to enhance the mastery of negotiation, it is helpful to practice on scenarios similar to those we are likely to encounter in business. This exercise deals with a potential strategic alliance with a supplier. The terminology and concepts are covered in Chapters 1 through 5.

The Gaylord Principle

The volatility of the paper market drives the wild fluctuations in price and availability. We are challenged with coming to an effective, long-term agreement (RELATIONSHIP) that will preserve our competitiveness and guarantee a steady supply stream of high-quality, reliable product (ISSUE). First, the six-point narrative.

1. Your company, Diversified United International (DUI), buys gaylords from three liner board mills. All three mills buy roll paper from the major forest products producers, then corrugate the board and convert to boxes.

2. Periodically, DUI reviews its requirements and seeks bids from suppliers. Qualitative experience with the suppliers, in terms of QSDP, is as follows:

Supplier	Quality	Service	Delivery	Price
Jiffy	Good	Great	Average	High
Miffy	Poor	Fair	Great	Low
Iffy	Inconsistent	Inconsistent	Inconsistent	Inconsistent

3. Another box supplier, the Gaylord Guy (GG), is only a converter. Until recently, GG bought liner board from Jiffy, Miffy, and Iffy (who are suspected of "carteling" the price) and converted the board to boxes. GG's quality, service and delivery are all great.

4. GG does well, plowing profits into expanded plant and equipment. He buys a corrugating machine to make his own board and buys roll paper from a mill that does not make liner board or boxes. GG has stopped buying board from "the cartel" and now competes directly with his former suppliers.

5. Additionally, GG has a deal with his roll paper supplier to make and sell boxes back to it (toll manufacturing or private label) for resale to that mill's markets. In return, GG receives a 15% price advantage on roll paper.

6. GG approaches DUI and offers a 10% price premium over the average price you are paying Jiffy, Miffy and Iffy. He justifies his higher price by his superior quality, service, and delivery, and he offers a money back guarantee. He wants all your box business.

Develop a strategy to address these practical matters

❖ List all the options that we have in choosing any supplier, or combination thereof, to purchase gaylords. State the reasons for each option, including the 'Do nothing' option.

❖ What do we know about GG's price (Price Analysis) and costs (Cost Analysis) that we can leverage into this situation? How does this affect our choice of tactics?

❖ Which type of negotiation strategy will we select? Choose

from Win-Win, Win-Lose, Lose-Win and Lose-Lose. State why your decision is justified.

❖ What are some possible motives that influence the thinking, and therefore perhaps the tactics, of DUI and GG?

❖ Write down how we will approach this negotiation.

> What is the ideal result?

> What points will we plan to concede?

• What are our HID and our cutoff points?

Use the Negotiation template on the next page to write a negotiation plan.

Negotiation Template

Strategy	Win-Win	Win-Lose	Lose-Win	Lose-Lose
Personality	Analytical	Practical	Amiable	Extrovert
Authority level				
Our Issues (known)	1	2	3	4
Our Positions (known)	**Quality**	**Service**	**Delivery**	**Price**
HID				
Nice				
Must				
Comments				
Their Issues (estimated)	1	2	3	4
Their Position (estimated)	**Quality**	**Service**	**Delivery**	**Price**
HID				
Nice				
Must				
Ideal Result				
Comments				
Our Concessions (expected)				
HID				
Nice				
Must				
Comments				
***Expected* Result**				
Comments				
What tactics do **we** expect to deploy?				
What tactics do we expect **them** to deploy?				
What was the final result?				
Other?				

The Gaylord Principle

Discussion of Possible Resolutions

No one solution fits all size problems, because as the buyer our goals depend upon our motivations. The number of Win-Win solutions to this question number as many as there are buyers and sellers. Here are some universally applicable considerations.

A. We know GG's positions. We must ascertain his motivations. They might include market share, competitor neutralization, pride, target customer or industry, cash flow, etc. Once GG's motives are established, decide how this fits into the buyer's goals.

   a. Why GG has made this market move at this time?

   b. What proportion of GG's book of business would our order represent?

   c. How will service, quality and delivery be assured and measured?

B. Identify and evaluate GG's costs. This step is crucial to obtaining the greatest value for the least total cost. We want to better our position. We are in no worse a position if we do not buy from GG, who also realizes our "security in doing nothing."

   a. How did GG determine a priced of 10% above its competitors?

   b. What relationship does GG's price bear to its costs?

   c. Will all our needs be met with GG, or must we source specialty items at a huge price premium?

   d. What percentage of our purchase volume are we willing to commit?

C. If GG and we intend to build a stable, long-term Win-Win relationship, we need to establish mutually favorable covenants. One approach is a modified Most Favored Nation (MFN) relationship in which GG agrees to sell to us at price, terms and conditions equal to (or incrementally better or worse) to those provided to GG's best customers.

D. GG may welcome this MFN approach because it wants to fill its basket with sales orders and then go looking to cherry-pick higher profit orders. Steel mills do this by lining up orders for basic product tonnages months in advance and use specialty steels for profit sweeteners or customer-negotiation bargaining chips.

E. Another form of strategic alliance is a shared savings or joint venture. Under this scenario, GG and we would benefit by economies generated by either party. Should we agree to purchase a certain volume per month, we occupy GG's machine production time, contributing to retiring GG's fixed costs. The relative magnitudes of GG's costs compared to the size and margin of our order affect the rate that GG makes on its investment. We can and should demand a share in the savings, which would otherwise accrue to GG (in an arm's length transaction) as higher profits.

F. Beware the 'money-back guarantee". It has high perceived value, but very low actual value. We are not interested in our money back because the dollar value of the boxes is a fraction of the amount of saleable product contained in each box shipped.

Moral of the story:

Always focus on reducing costs. Consider sharing the savings with strategic partners.

Appendix B

Adults learn best by doing. After reading Chapters 3, 4 and 5, jump right in and tackle this exercise in creating a negotiation plan. The two separate sections reflect the fact that purchasing departments often must negotiate with internal customers (The Cowboys) and the supplier (The Indians).

Fighting the Cowboys and the Indians

(At the Same Time)

Narrative*:*

This negotiation exercise concerns a major high-tech procurement project. Executive management has directed that Purchasing is to do all procurement. All existing suppliers have been advised and have signed off on this policy.

Nevertheless, a request from the MIS/IT folks arrives at Purchasing in the form of a requisition needing a PO number and authorized signature. The justification of MIS/IT is that Purchasing adds very little value to high-tech procurement because Purchasing has little in-depth knowledge of the discipline. Besides, this is the usual way that business has been conducted.

The products and services purchased under the proposed contract are for promising new and Alpha-tested, but unproven technology. Moreover, no time remains for Purchasing to mess with the order and the supplier has already committed resources and incurred substantial costs at the authorization of the MIS/IT folks.

Our examination of the proposed contract shows that the

statement of work is unclear and subject to interpretation.

Deliverables and timetables are sketchy, and no language exists as to enforceability or remedies. We are unwilling to place our signature on the document and consider seeking the approval of executive management.

The supplier is new to us and, in fact, new to business as a unit. Two executives who formed the company left a previous employer, a supplier with whom we have some overall good but not spectacular experience. The other principal of the new supplier is a stranger to us and has not participated much in the project with MIS/IT in the technical phase, just in the "contract stage."

We have two challenges here.

1. Negotiate an effective and long-term agreement (RELATIONSHIP) that will preserve our competitiveness and guarantee a steady stream of high-quality, reliable technical information and services (ISSUE) with the supplier.

2. Confront the source of the first problem, our own internal customer. We would like to prohibit this mistake from happening again.

Part One – Cowboys (The Internal Customer)

We are presented with a potential prescription for disaster as has happened before under similar circumstances. MIS/IT folks do not understand the process and value of professional purchasing, and they have enjoyed the independence and power of avoiding Purchasing. They obviously do not see how their rosy view of the supplier and its product/service may not bear up under Purchasing's scrutiny, let alone provide for long-term performance.

Formulate answers to these questions:

1. What is our strategy for approaching MIS/IT?

2. What is our alternative to approaching MIS/IT?

3. Are we willing to have them walk away?

4. What about avoiding them entirely and just throwing the requisition out?

5. How would we persuade them of the wisdom of getting us on board early in the procurement process?

6. What measures could we use to convince them of cooperation in this matter?

7. Will this negotiation be a Win-Win? How so?

8. What is our negotiation strategy?

9. What tactics will we deploy?

10. What steps will we take to ensure this does not happen again?

11. What deliverables are they looking for?

12. What metrics will we use to determine if we got what we wanted/bought?

13. What are the timetable breakouts that they want, and what deliverables are due to them?

14. What is our concession strategy?

15. What concessions do we expect to make?

16. How and when do we plan to make them?

17. What concessions do we expect them to make?

18. What else can we anticipate?

Part Two – Indians (The Supplier)

The supplier may not be completely innocent because he knows that he should deal with the buyer but prefers the back-door sales approach, as he does with many other customers and has with us in the past. If we stay with this supplier, we will need to revise the proposed contract form and most of the Terms and Conditions. Since this supplier is not on the qualified list, we have much investigating to do.

Formulate answers to these questions:

1. What is our strategy for approaching the supplier?

2. Why should this supplier deal with us at all?

3. What is our alternative to approaching this supplier?

4. Are we willing to have them walk away?

5. What about avoiding them entirely and sourcing elsewhere?

6. How will we handle these concerns?

     a. Financial

     b. Insurance

     c. Patent infringement

7. What steps will we take to ensure this does not happen again?

8. What enforceability provisions can we insert?

9. What other provisions do we want to insert into the contract?

10. How can we tie performance to payment?

11. How can we ensure payment, performance, and other protections in the contract?

12. Will this negotiation be a Win-Win? Why or why not and how?

13. What is our negotiation strategy?

14. What tactics will we deploy?

15. What is our concession strategy?

16. What concessions do we expect to make?

17. How and when do we plan to make them?

18. What concessions do we expect them to make?

19. What else can we anticipate?

Refer to the Negotiation template in Appendix A.

Appendix C

Everyone wants to know more about negotiation tactics. This bonus list cites another dozen and one-half tactics, the use of which as described here, clearly identify one as an amateur in negotiation.

The Amateur Negotiator's Tactics

In 1979, Royal Little, the 83-year old founder of Textron and father of the modern conglomerate, wrote a book titled, "How To Lose $100,000,000 And Other Valuable Information." It chronicled some of his colossal business failures, and how he learned from them. Mr. Little kept a picture in his office of the yacht on which his company lost millions as a symbol of his foolish mistakes. His point was that it is often far more beneficial in business to study what not to do. I agree. And it is far cheaper to learn from the mistakes of others.

Borrowing from that wisdom, let's examine what mistakes to avoid in negotiation. This list of top boners, while no means exhaustive, does highlight many common errors. See if you can find any of your favorites in the list.

1. ***Accepting the first offer***. If you do, it will drive you nuts. How do you know that you could not have done better? You will suffer a bad case of buyer's remorse in no time. Negotiation is a process in which skipping steps leads to tripping on them.

2. ***Being the first to name the price***. This violates the TCO philosophy and sets the stage for an auction where price is all that matters. Kodak sells priceless memories, not low-

priced film. Sales people are trying to establish value before setting a price. We want to identify all the elements of cost. We will get to the price in due time.

3. ***Falling in love with the deal***. Do you love your spouse? Your kids? Your pets? Then why would you ever consider loving anything that cannot love you back? This trait is not all bad, because it represents our devotion to duty. Do not let that emotional investment take over rational thinking.

4. ***Divulging your time frame***. The likelihood of foolish and expensive decisions increases as the amount of lead-time decreases. In the early 1980's, I imported construction technology from Europe. After many meetings in the US and several trips to Europe, I decided that the time was right to close the deal, so off I went to France. Promptly upon arrival, I announced to my hosts that I was there for only four days. We had much to do and I expected to leave with a completed deal. For three days, we negotiated in circles until it all fell apart. On the ride to the airport, my hosts assured me that we could still do the deal, if I only I would be "a little more reasonable." They got more out of me in those last 20 minutes than in the whole year we had known each other. Looking back, I could have stayed on for another month, struck a more favorable deal, and been a whole lot better off. Instead, I lost by trapping myself in my own time frame.

5. ***Leaving issues dangling***. This habit encourages discontent and invites renegotiation. Some personality types shun resolution so that the issues are always available to pull back out at the first provocation. Resolve the straggler issues, adopt measures to ensure they cannot be resurrected as bargaining points, and move on.

6. ***Going for the kill***. Suppose you miss? Do you really need the extra enemy? Resolve to leave egos, dignity, and wallets intact when you leave the table. You will not have another Win-Win opportunity if the other party is out of business.

7. ***Ignoring conflict***. Conflict in negotiation is inevitable. Each party has something that the other wants! Rule 1 tells us that negotiation requires and resolves conflict, so why

ignore the elephant in the living room?

8. ***Talking about people, not issues***. This is an unforgivable mistake. Ad hominem attacks never accomplish anything good, no matter how justified. Focus on the problem and how to resolve it. Let your knowledge of personalities and communication skills dictate your approach to the people problems.

9. ***Ending on a sour note***. Mutual satisfaction requires mutual commitment. If one side feels cheated or unsatisfied, how much can we count on their commitment to the negotiated deal?

10. ***Missing a Win-Win opportunity***. If a Win-Win outcome is possible, it is worth the extra effort and time to achieve it. Selfishness or greed breeds a culture of resentment that will unleash its revenge at the first opportunity.

11. ***Inadequate preparation***. We devoted two chapters to preparation. The lion's share of the time is in researching and planning. Mountains of information and an organized plan of attack are the hallmarks of the successful negotiator.

12. ***Arguing!*** Save that for the lawyers. Negotiation involves only two reasonable and willing parties. If your negotiation efforts and skills fail, you'll have plenty of time to add an expensive third-party litigant.

13. ***Impatience***. This is a weapon we often donate as a free gift for the other side to use against us. If our impatience is caused by lack of preparation, or advancing deadline, we have another problem. Otherwise, be prepared to listen patiently. Stalling is an instinctive tactic when the other side senses impatience.

14. ***Threatening***. You can often tip your hand on strategy by threatening alternative actions. Take a clue from Washington diplomats who never rule any option in or out, and thus never threaten anything. If they announced their military preparedness, for instance, they might unwittingly put their forces in harm's way.

15. **Belittling and Grandstanding**. There is never any room for this in professional negotiations. It is a clear lack of respect and invites retaliation. You would not be at the table if you did not want something, so why make it harder for yourself?

16. **Having no written negotiation plan**. Winging it is a sure nosedive to failure.

17. **Forgetting the 10-10-10 Rule**. Business folks understand the value of a customer. This is why most will lose the battle and the money in a dispute if the relationship can be salvaged. For a seller with an irate customer, it takes 10 minutes to lose the customer, 10 months to replace the customer and costs 10 times as much as keeping the original customer. That is the 10-10-10 rule and it may be worth reminding a wayward supplier from time to time.

18. **Not having a Dutch Uncle Speech**. The Dutch Uncle is the mythical figure that admonishes sternly, bluntly, but with sincerity and kindness. From time to time, it becomes necessary to remind a recalcitrant supplier that it is in our mutual best interests to solve the problems besetting us. Otherwise, we may not continue to do business together, which is not a welcome prospect to either of us.

The good news is that not making these mistakes in the course of your everyday commerce will vastly improve your negotiation skills. The better news is that it doesn't cost $100,000,000 to learn them!

Index

U

UCC, 105, 106, 107, 108, 109, 115, 116
Ultimatum, 104, 126
Uniform Commercial Code (UCC), 105
Union(s), 56

V

Verbal eraser, 78
Verbal language, 78
Verbal Language, 78

W

Walk away (out), 131, 144, 146
Wall Street Journal, 3, 32, 86
Wife, iii, 80, 99, 100, 133
WIIFM (What's In It For Me?), 94, 99
Win-Lose, 1, 5, 63, 65, 66, 67, 71, 120, 124, 125, 129, 139, 140
Win-Win, 4, 7, 13, 61, 62, 63, 65, 66, 68, 69, 71, 72, 91, 112, 113, 120, 125, 131, 139, 140, 141, 145, 146, 148, 149
Writing, 24, 50, 74, 86, 87, 92, 102

X

Y

Z

Zantac, 27, 28

To order additional copies of this book...

Simply visit
www.YouNegotiateIt.com

Order multiple copies of this book and receive discounted prices. Other products by Robert A. Menard II such as CD's on Negotiation, major speeches to conventions, reprints of his many magazine articles, and new releases are also available.

For multiple copies of "You're the Buyer – You Negotiate It" shipped together to the same address, the following discounts apply:

2 to 5 copies	5% savings	$17.00 each
6 to 25 copies	10% savings	$16.00 each
26 to 50 copies	15% savings	$15.00 each
51 or more	20% savings	$14.00 each

Shipping and handling costs decrease per unit for larger orders. Texas sales taxes apply. Expedited shipping is available.

Payment must accompany order. Major credit cards accepted.

Prices and discounts subject to change.